A STITCH IN TIME: HELPING YOUNG MOTHERS COMPLETE HIGH SCHOOL

Elizabeth A. McGee

with

Susan Blank

Academy for Educational Development
1989

Library of Congress Catalog Card Number 90-30197
ISBN 0-89492-068-5

TABLE OF CONTENTS

APPENDIX

FOREWORD

A *Stitch in Time* is the second publication developed by the Academy for Educational Development's (AED's) Support Center for Educational Equity for Young Mothers. The Support Center was established to serve as a resource to policymakers, practitioners, and service providers working to improve educational opportunities for women who began childbearing before graduating from high school. Staff at the Center conduct research, produce reports, provide training and offer technical assistance.

The Support Center is a project of the School and Community Services division of AED. This division is committed to a notion of educational reform that stresses both excellence and equity. Much of its work focuses on four primary objectives:

- improving the access of poor youth to educationally sound programs
- reducing school dropout rates
- preventing adolescent pregnancy
- improving school-to-work transitions

In all of these areas, AED works with schools and community service organizations to strengthen opportunities for educationally and economically disadvantaged youth. Recognizing the larger social and economic context that puts students at risk of school failure and eventual unemployment, we emphasize improving policies, structures and practices of schools and school systems so that they can develop effective institutional responses to the problems these students encounter as learners. We seek not only to help individual schools improve but also to foster collaborations between schools and community-based organizations serving youth. Such partnerships often make responses possible that no single school could undertake on its own.

It is, then, with a sense of great urgency that AED has undertaken improving educational opportunities for pregnant and parenting teens, a population whose needs, research has shown, have too often been ignored or inadequately addressed by many school districts. Assisting young mothers to complete their educations will have a positive impact, not only on their lives but also on those of their children. We believe that *A Stitch in Time* combines an analysis of the complex factors involved in teenage parenthood with clear recommendations for policy and program change. We hope it will become a useful resource for concerned educators and service providers seeking to develop programs and strategies responsive to the needs of pregnant and parenting students.

The major writer of *A Stitch in Time* is Elizabeth A. McGee, an expert in the area of teenage pregnancy. Ms. McGee has contributed to many publications on adolescent sexuality and childbearing, including *Changing Bodies, Changing Lives: A Book for Teens on Sex and Relationships.*

Two people have been crucial in allowing AED to pursue its work on behalf of these students. They are Edward J. Meade, Jr. and Shelby H. Miller, Program Officers at the Ford Foundation, without whose concern, guidance and generous support, much of AED's work in this area would not have been possible.

Michele Cahill
Vice President and Director
School and Community Services
Academy for Educational Development

ACKNOWLEDGMENTS

Many people contributed time and expertise to this report. I want to thank the staff of the School and Community Services Division of the Academy for Educational Development for their generosity with support and suggestions. Several staff members were especially helpful. Appreciation begins with Michele Cahill, Vice President and Director of School and Community Services, who early on asked the right questions and whose wisdom, patience, and sensitivity to the challenges facing schools have been invaluable. Elayne Archer helped to shape the report's organization and argument. Patrick Montesano provided a thoughtful review of the final draft. Aurelia Enache skillfully and cheerfully managed long hours of preparing the manuscript for printing. Sandy Weinbaum held me to a high standard for describing the lives of teenage mothers. Anne Galletta shepherded the report through the printing phase of production. Melody Brooks, Michelle Sajous, and Paula Vincent assisted with still other aspects of producing the report.

A number of colleagues reviewed an earlier draft of this report and were both kind and astute in recommending improvements. I am grateful to Margaret Dunkle, Katherine Fennelly, Eileen Hayes, Jeanne Lindsay, James McCarthy, Alice Radosh, Lisa Syron, Joan Tigue, and Constancia Warren. In addition to reviewing a draft of the report, Joy Dryfoos shared her tremendous research knowledge and spent hours tracking down and analyzing data cited here.

Susan Blank edited the manuscript and made a critical contribution to the way the material is presented and analyzed. Her diligence and good sense are reflected throughout this report. Dore Hollander did a careful job of copyediting which also improved the report significantly.

Waldon Press was responsible for typesetting and printing. I appreciate the personal attention William Donat, President of Waldon Press, gave to this publication.

Elizabeth A. McGee

PREFACE

Lilia is 17, in the fourth month of her junior year of high school, and five months pregnant. She has just confided to her Home Economics teacher that she is going to leave school and marry her 19-year-old boyfriend, who works as a security guard at a local shopping mall. Lilia's teacher thinks she should attend the district's program for pregnant students, but the program is across town — eight miles from her home, which Lilia thinks is too far. Lilia believes that after the baby is born, her family and husband will want her to stay at home.

*   *   *

Keesha, who had been held back a year in school, was 15 when she became pregnant during the second semester of eighth grade. She transferred to a program for pregnant girls and returned to ninth grade at her local high school when her baby was just a few weeks old. She managed to complete her sophomore year with an adequate academic record. While she attended school for that year, Keesha's mother cared for her child. However, now the child is two, and Keesha's mother says she can no longer baby-sit. Keesha cannot afford child care to fit her school schedule, and since she is of the age when she can leave school legally, she is not planning to return to school. She still sees the father of her baby, and his family tries to help her. With their baby-sitting assistance, she hopes to enroll in an equivalency certificate program, but sometimes she thinks it would be better for her child if she stayed home.

*   *   *

When Melanie, 18, came to the county hospital about eight hours before her son was born, it was only her third pregnancy-related visit to any health facility. Melanie last attended school in the tenth grade. She has been living with the father of her child for a year, and although the relationship is stormy, she believes that she will marry him. While she works behind the counter at a local bakery — a job she has held for nearly a year — Melanie leaves her baby with an older sister, who has two children. Melanie wants

1

a high school diploma, but she thinks she is too far behind in academic subjects and too busy with her job and homemaking to succeed in a General Equivalency Degree (GED) preparation course.

*   *   *

This book is for educators and community activists who want to help young women like Lilia, Keesha, and Melanie acquire something they badly need — a high school diploma. As these brief profiles suggest, students who are pregnant or have children present heavily burdened schools and school districts with a web of complex problems and potential new responsibilities. Yet, as will be argued in the following pages, it is critical that schools work with other agencies to help young mothers and mothers-to-be untangle enough of those problems so that they can finish their secondary education. Surprisingly, given the surge of attention to adolescent parenthood over the past 10 years, relatively little has been done thus far to address *systematically* the obstacles to completing high school in a timely manner that pregnant and parenting teenagers face. This book attempts to advance that work.

INTRODUCTION

Fewer teenagers bear children today than did so in the past. In the United States, birthrates for adolescents in all but the youngest age groups have been declining for decades and reached a record low in 1986.[1] Nevertheless, young mothers have attracted considerable attention in recent years, in part because other changes have made them an especially vulnerable group.

One of the changes has been a downward shift in the age at which teenagers become mothers. While it is still uncommon for adolescents younger than 15 to have sexual intercourse, the proportion of youngsters doing so has increased; as a result birthrates have not declined among girls aged 10-14 as they have for teenagers who are older.[2] Thus, a larger proportion of today's adolescent mothers are younger than was the case in previous decades, and in comparison to those in other Western industrialized countries, many American teenage mothers are extremely young.[3]

Another change has been in the marital status of teen mothers: increasingly, they are single. The source of this change is a complex interaction of several trends: the proportion of teenagers who are single has increased, and the rate of childbearing among this group has risen. At the same time, the proportion of teenagers who are married has decreased, and their rate of childbearing has declined. Overall, more than 60% of today's births to teenagers are to unmarried women — a rate that has doubled since 1970.[4] With such a large proportion of young mothers bearing children outside of marriage, and with another sizable group becoming divorced (rates of

1. James Trussell, "Teenage Pregnancy in the United States," *Family Planning Perspectives* (Vol. 20, No. 6, Nov./Dec. 1988).
2. Karen Pittman and Gina Adams, *Teenage Pregnancy: An Advocate's Guide to the Numbers* (Washington, DC: Children's Defense Fund, 1988).
3. Elise F. Jones et al., *Teenage Pregnancy in Industrialized Countries* (New Haven: Yale University Press, 1988).
4. Pittman and Adams, op. cit. (see note 2).

marital dissolution are higher for teens than for adults[5]), women who give birth to their first child as teenagers are likely to be the sole support of their families for significant periods of time.

Yet changes in the economy have made it increasingly difficult for young adults to find jobs that pay enough to support a family.[6] As teen mothers often lack the educational preparation necessary for such jobs, they are particularly likely to become part of the growing population of young parents who have trouble making ends meet. Not surprisingly, then, many young mothers struggle with poverty, often alternating between work and welfare for years.

A final change in the status of today's teenage mothers is that they may live in more deprived social environments relative to other teenagers than was the case for adolescent mothers in previous decades. Contemporary teenagers have had greater access to both contraception and abortion than their predecessors. One reason some girls who become mothers do not avail themselves of these options is that new restrictions on access to reproductive health care services have disproportionately affected poor young women. However, it is also possible that some young women do not use the available birth control methods because they are less hopeful about their future than their peers are. Supporting this hypothesis is the fact that teenagers who are not college-bound are more likely to have a baby now than they were two decades ago — an increase that has been particularly pronounced for young black women.[7] For these reasons and others, birthrates for disadvantaged girls are 4-8 times those of advantaged teens.[8]

Although the social and economic circumstances of teen mothers have worsened, society's response to their problems has improved somewhat. Teen mothers' legal right to an education was established with the passage of Title IX of the Education Amendments of 1972, which forbids discrim-

---

5. Maris A. Vinovskis and P. Lindsay Chase-Lansdale, "Should We Discourage Teenage Marriage?" *Public Interest* (No. 87, Spring 1987).

Frank Furstenberg, Jr., "Bringing Back the Shotgun Wedding," *Public Interest* (No. 90, Winter 1988).

6. William T. Grant Foundation Commission on Work, Family, and Citizenship, *The Forgotten Half: Non-College Youth in America* (Washington, DC: 1988).

7. Frank L. Mott and Nan L. Maxwell, "School-Age Mothers: 1968 and 1979," *Family Planning Perspectives* (Vol. 13, No. 6, Nov./Dec. 1981).

8. Joy Dryfoos, Hastings-on-Hudson, NY, personal communication, 1989.

ination against pregnant and parenting students.[9] While school districts were once free to expel these students, since 1975, when the Title IX regulations went into effect, the most blatant forms of such discrimination have decreased. In fact, as we shall see, many school districts have actively taken steps to respond to the needs of pregnant and parenting teenagers. This response has taken various forms, including special programs for pregnant students, school-based child care centers, and courses tailored to new parents.

Yet, however helpful, these efforts have reached only a fraction of the young women who need support. Few school districts have developed a systemwide approach for identifying and assisting pregnant and parenting teenagers who have not finished high school, and few schools have organized a plan for retaining or re-enrolling these students. In some communities, informal networks of staff in schools and service agencies have created an ad hoc system to help pregnant students, but once these students give birth, there is far less support for their completing school on time — or at all.

Thus, progress in meeting Title IX's mandate of equal rights for pregnant and parenting students has been limited.[10] For example, pregnant and parenting students are neglected in most of the new dropout prevention and at-risk youth initiatives that have been developed across the country.[11] Although childbearing is common among female dropouts and interest in preventing long-term welfare dependency among teenage mothers is widespread, most states or school districts with new dropout prevention plans direct only a very small proportion of their funds for these programs to students who are pregnant or mothers. A recent study of 47 model programs serving school dropouts or youth at risk of dropping out found that

9. Margaret Dunkle, *Adolescent Pregnancy and Parenting: Evaluating School Policies and Programs from a Sex Equity Perspective* (Washington, DC: Council of Chief State School Officers, 1985).

Gail L. Zellman, *A Title IX Perspective on the School's Response to Teenage Pregnancy and Parenthood* (Santa Monica, CA: Rand Corporation, 1981).

10. Margaret A. Nash and Margaret Dunkle, *The Need for a Warming Trend: A Survey of the School Climate for Pregnant and Parenting Teens* (Washington, DC: Equality Center, 1989).

11. Academy for Educational Development, *Improving Educational Opportunities for Pregnant and Parenting Students* (New York: 1988).

only three of these programs were specifically designed to assist pregnant and parenting adolescents.[12]

The failure to ensure that pregnant students and those with children have the support they need to finish their education suggests that, despite changes in the law, many old attitudes about them persist. Often their problems are considered personal and not the responsibility of the schools. An administrator described how this attitude manifests itself in one urban school district: "These kids don't exist for our district. The attitude of school personnel is that school-age parents don't belong to us. There's such a mindset against them — in effect, our school people are saying to these girls, 'You've made your bed; now lie in it.'"[13]

Attitudes toward pregnant students and students who are mothers are also affected by the fact that, in many communities, teenage pregnancy is a divisive issue. The controversies that surround adolescent childbearing sometimes seem so potentially disruptive that educators shy away from focusing on the obstacles young mothers-to-be and mothers encounter in trying to complete school. As one educator recently observed, "People think that if we help pregnant students, we're advocating teenage sex, and if we help student mothers, we're rewarding 'bad girls'".[14]

The case for doing more to help teenage mothers finish their secondary school education rests on humane, legal, and practical considerations. Many of these young women must become the breadwinners for their families, and if we care at all about them and their children, we will quickly recognize that graduation from high school is an important first step to economic self-sufficiency. From a legal perspective, young mothers are entitled to a fair share of the many dollars now being spent to help students who have traditionally been alienated from school. Indeed, ignoring pregnant and parenting dropouts in such funding allocations is discriminatory. As a practical matter, we pay high social costs for neglecting young parents' educational needs. The economic hardship faced by teen mothers who de-

---

12. Claire D. Brindis and Rita J. Jeremy, *Adolescent Pregnancy and Parenting in California: A Strategic Plan for Action* (San Francisco, CA: Institute for Health Policy Studies, University of California, 1988).

13. Support Center for Educational Equity for Young Mothers, Field notes from a Survey of Policies, Practices, Programs, and Plans for Pregnant and Parenting Students in Nine Urban School Districts (New York: Academy for Educational Development, 1988).

14. Ibid.

lay completing or fail to complete high school places a great strain on public service systems. Furthermore, a mother's level of educational attainment affects her children's level of achievement; a dropout thus leaves her children especially vulnerable to school failure.

A final reason to focus on young mothers' education is that contained within one of the recent reforms in the welfare program, Aid to Families with Dependent Children (AFDC), is a new education mandate directed toward teenage mothers.[15] AFDC parents under age 20 without a high school diploma are required to participate in an education program regardless of the age of their youngest child. Considerable debate surrounds the merit of this requirement. Nevertheless, in response to the new legislation, public agencies, including school districts, will have to concentrate more on the educational needs of teenage mothers on welfare.

Many of the policies and practices that school districts must adopt to help young welfare mothers would also help teenage mothers who do not receive AFDC and other students who are at risk of not completing high school. Indeed, pregnant and parenting teenagers are in many ways typical of a large group of students for whom high school education, as currently structured, does not work. These students need a wider range of educational choices.[16] They would benefit from the opportunity to select from a greater number of educational settings and approaches; furthermore, they might have better success in schools with more flexible schedules, a shorter instructional day, more experiential learning, programs that combine education and work, and policies that would make closer relationships with caring adults a more common feature of the school experience. One other reason, then, to pursue educational reforms on behalf of young mothers is that these changes are intrinsically part of a basic strategy to keep students in school. At the same time, since some young women turn to parenthood as a socially sanctioned means of avoiding school, increasing the number of students who feel positively about school promises to reduce the appeal of early childbearing.

However compelling the case for more systematic efforts to help teenage

15. American Public Welfare Association et al., *New Partnerships: Education's Stake in the Family Support Act of 1988* (Washington, DC: William T. Grant Foundation Commission, 1989).

16. Gary Lacy, Cliff Johnson, and David Heffernan, *Tackling the Youth Employment Problem* (Washington, DC: Children's Defense Fund, 1989).

mothers complete their education, it is important to be realistic about the potential benefits of these strategies. Factors other than early childbearing also are responsible for young mothers' poor educational outcomes. A combination of socioeconomic, family, and personal characteristics make certain children very vulnerable to having problems later in life. When schools and other youth-serving institutions do not meet their needs, many of these children later make choices, such as early childbearing, that exacerbate their difficulties. To counter these difficulties, services for young mothers may have to be more intensive and of greater duration than services for other dropouts and potential dropouts.

Similarly, high school graduation by no means guarantees that young mothers will enjoy economic well-being: factors other than educational level play an important role in determining their prospects for self-sufficiency. Many high school graduates cannot support a family on their earnings alone. Also, like other mothers in our society, women who give birth as teenagers face a variety of obstacles to success in the labor market. For example, because mothers are less likely to work in the years immediately after giving birth, they have difficulty acquiring the employment skills and work experience that will help them attain well-paid jobs when they enter the labor force. Furthermore, the earning potential of mothers is undercut by the subordinate position of women in the labor market and by our society's failure to offer more than a modicum of support to working parents. These problems are compounded when a mother tries to support herself and her children without financial help from a partner.

Notwithstanding these very real difficulties, if more is done to help teenage mothers earn diplomas, it should be possible to reduce the years of floundering and economic hardship that too many of them now face. Indeed, whatever their problems, many adolescents who begin childbearing before they graduate from high school eventually continue their education and acquire a diploma or an equivalency certificate. In view of the capacity of these mothers to combine schooling and motherhood, there is good reason to believe that the investment of extra support from schools and other institutions could make the critical difference in enabling more young mothers to complete their secondary education and to do so in a timely fashion. When young mothers are actively involved in an educational program, they are not only more likely to finish high school but also more likely to delay subsequent childbearing.

8

*   *   *

Educators and others active in adolescent pregnancy issues can be part of an effort to reduce the obstacles to school enrollment and completion among young mothers-to-be and mothers in their community. To address the educational needs of these students more effectively, they should recruit other individuals who share their concerns and follow this three-step process: first, marshal facts as to why young women who have a baby before graduating from high school need better educational opportunities. Second, develop the case for why current approaches to helping pregnant and parenting teenagers with their schooling are inadequate. Third, press for change in the school district or in individual schools. This report is designed to help with these steps.

A Stitch in Time is also intended to fill a gap in the literature on teenage mothers and education. It presents an overview of previous research and summarizes information gathered through a survey conducted by staff of the Academy for Educational Development's Support Center for Educational Equity for Young Mothers. Building on this information, the report then provides practical advice on how educators can work with youth-service providers and community activists to reduce the institutional barriers that keep pregnant and parenting teens from remaining in or returning to a diploma-granting educational program or GED program.

The title of this report may lead some readers to assume that it will address pregnancy prevention. While schools have an important role to play in helping all students avoid pregnancy, this report is concerned only with strengthening the capacity of educational institutions to help young mothers avoid additional unplanned pregnancies and other problems that interfere with their schooling.

Chapters 1 and 2 offer a review of what is known about the current situation of pregnant and parenting students and how schools and school districts are responding to them. As one school administrator recently observed, "I rely on research and statistics to prove that reforms for such a controversial group as teenage parents are needed."[17] The final chapter offers guidelines on how to initiate a districtwide or school-based strategy for helping young mothers complete high school.

This report focuses on action at the local level. Nevertheless, federal and

---

17. Support Center for Educational Equity for Young Mothers, op. cit. (see note 13).

state policymaking are also important.[18] Improvements in federal and state policies would strengthen and expand schools' assistance to pregnant and parenting students. For example, school districts would be more effective in re-enrolling dropouts if home visitors were available to help young mothers plan for their return to school. Similarly, districts could do more to help student mothers stay in school if they could ensure them access to various kinds of child care, including family day care and school-based care. Finally, districts could reduce the likelihood that homelessness will interfere with a young mother's school attendance if there were more affordable housing for young families.

A limitation of this report is that it does not directly consider teenage fathers. Young mothers are usually the custodial parents or primary care givers for their children, so typically it is they, not the young fathers, who must contend with the conflicts between child care and schooling. Nonetheless, some young fathers are helping to rear their offspring and face conflicts between pursuing their education and earning money to contribute to the support of their child. Therefore, young fathers, like young mothers, would benefit from programs that offer students with significant home responsibilities new ways to meet personal and academic obligations. Though not specified as such, many of the changes discussed in this report also speak to the educational needs of young fathers.

Helping teenage mothers when they are young will, in many cases, help set them on the path to self-sufficiency, lessening their need for extensive assistance when they are older. The improvement in their prospects will, in turn, have a positive effect on their children, our next generation of students. A stitch in time saves nine.

---

18. Constancia Warren, *Meeting the Educational Needs of Pregnant and Parenting Adolescents: Recommendations for State Action* (New York: Center for Public Advocacy Research, 1990).

CHAPTER ONE

THE LIVES OF TEENAGE MOTHERS

This chapter provides an overview of information on the number of teenage mothers, their possible motivations for early childbearing, their marital and fertility patterns, their levels of educational attainment and school enrollment patterns, and their prospects for financial stability. A good working knowledge of the characteristics of teenage mothers is essential to mobilizing support for change. Just as important, new approaches for assisting them with education should be rooted in a realistic assessment of their needs.

Much of the data summarized in this chapter describe *all* teenage mothers, not the group of young mothers who are of primary concern in this book — those who begin childbearing before they complete high school. Unfortunately, there is not enough research isolating this smaller group. But information on a subset of teenagers who make up a significant proportion of the mothers without high school diplomas — girls who have children when they are younger than 18 is available: on average, these young mothers come from circumstances that are far more problematic than those of teenagers who are older when they first give birth.[19] If more information were available, it would probably be apparent that most young women who give birth before they graduate are living in more disadvantaged circumstances and facing more serious obstacles to achieving personal and economic stability than are those who have finished high school by the time they bear their first child.

At the same time, it is important to recognize that even teen mothers who have not graduated are not a monolithic group. These young women differ from one another in age, marital status, levels of scholastic achievement,

19. Dawn Upchurch and James McCarthy, "Adolescent Childbearing and High School Completion: Have Things Changed?" (Baltimore: Department of Population Dynamics, Johns Hopkins School of Hygiene and Public Health, 1989).

school status, geographic location, and family background; and these differences have important implications for their subsequent schooling.

Early Childbearing: Black and White

Before reviewing the research on teenage parenthood, it is important to note that investigators often present their findings by comparing racial and ethnic differences among teenagers. However, this practice can limit our understanding of adolescent childbearing. While most research indicates that several distinctive racial and ethnic variables affect both the probability of teenagers' becoming mothers and the nature of their subsequent experiences, evidence also indicates that focusing on race and ethnicity can obscure the importance of other variables, particularly socioeconomic status and its correlates.

For instance, the fact that birthrates for nonwhite teenagers are double those for whites has attracted a great deal of publicity; yet if we compare young women who come from families with similar incomes and who have comparable levels of educational achievement, differences in birthrates for white, black, and Hispanic teenagers disappear. Thus, one in five poor teens with lower-than-average basic academic skills is a mother — and this is equally true for whites, blacks, and Hispanics.[20] This analysis should remind us that comparing statistics on early childbearing for teens of different ethnic or racial backgrounds can reinforce stereotypes. Therefore, in this report such comparisons are used only to draw attention to issues that deserve special consideration or to present research findings accurately.

Number of Teenage Mothers

Approximately 463,000 teenagers will give birth in 1989.[21] This estimate includes young women who are having their first child as well as those who are giving birth to their second or third child. However, the overall number of teenage mothers will be much larger than the number giving birth because many young women who already have children will still be teenagers.

Currently, an estimated 900,000 young women under the age of 20 are

20. Pittman and Adams, op. cit. (see note 2).
21. Trussell, op. cit. (see note 1).

mothers — about one in 10 of all teenage females.[22] Two-thirds of these mothers are 18 and 19 years of age, and the remainder are 17 years old or younger.

Rates of adolescent childbearing are far higher in the United States than in other industrialized countries.[23] If the birthrates that were recorded for American teenagers in 1985 continue to prevail, one-fifth of today's young women will have had one or more births by their 20th birthday.[24] Furthermore, the proportion of young women living in low-income families who will have had children by the time they are 20 is likely to greatly exceed the national average.

Motivations for Early Childbearing

Stereotypes about teenage mothers abound, and almost all of them are negative. Young women who start childbearing during their teenage years are often portrayed as girls with problems, adolescents seeking love in an inappropriate way, or young people with a welfare mentality. In order to see these young mothers more realistically, we must examine the kinds of conclusions drawn by researchers who have studied the causes and consequences of teenage childbearing.

Many of the early studies of teenage mothers tried to isolate the psychological characteristics of adolescents who become unwed mothers. However, this kind of analysis leads to an oversimplification of the causes of early childbearing. A more accurate view of adolescent childbearing does not ignore the part that psychological factors play in a teenager's decision to bear children: that decision may well be a way of bolstering feelings of competence and independence — a psychological need that is shared by all adolescents. But the more important difference between adolescents who become mothers and those who delay motherhood is that most of the former come from circumstances in which the typical routes to developing an adult sense of self — school success, earning money, planning for college or a career, marriage — are unusually constricted.

As evidence for this conclusion, a number of scholars point to common

---

22. Dryfoos, op. cit. (see note 8).
23. Jones et al., op. cit. (see note 3).
24. Stanley Henshaw and Jennifer Van Vort, "Teenage Abortion, Birth, and Pregnancy Statistics: An Update," *Family Planning Perspectives* (Vol. 21, No. 2, Mar./ Apr. 1989).

features in the lives of adolescents who become mothers. For instance, the vast majority of these teens come from families with low or modest incomes: three-quarters of all women under the age of 20 who give birth are from families that are poor or close to poor.[25] Many also live in racially isolated neighborhoods. Furthermore, even before conceiving, teenage mothers ranked much lower than their classmates in scholastic performance.[26] Indeed, many were behind grade level in their schoolwork, and a significant proportion had dropped out of school before becoming pregnant.[27] Finally, a disproportionate number of teenage mothers have grown up, in whole or in part, in single-parent families.[28]

Of course, many adolescents with these same background characteristics manage to avoid early childbearing because other influences — for instance, a positive relationship with a parent or other significant adult — lessen the effects of these well- established risk factors for teenage parenthood.[29] Still, the most important factors underlying early childbearing appear to be the social environment created by poverty and the problems that follow in its wake. The difficulties of struggling to make ends meet in a society where many are affluent take their toll on both parents and children in low-income families. To make matters worse, many of these families send their children to schools that lack the resources to meet students' needs, and these families cannot afford, or do not have the time or skills, to supplement their children's education outside of school. For many of these children, unsatisfactory school experiences, compounded by the expectation that the jobs awaiting workers without a postsecondary education will be low-paying and frustrating, drain them of faith in the future and, for the girls, lead them to look to parenthood as an alternative source of satisfaction.

In other words, many young women facing bleak personal circumstances perceive that there is little to be lost and perhaps something to be

---

25. Trussell, op. cit. (see note 1).

26. Gus W. Haggstrom et al., *Teenage Parents: Their Situations and Attainments* (Santa Monica, CA: Rand Corporation, 1981).

27. Denise F. Polit and Janet R. Kahn, *"Teenage Pregnancy and the Role of the Schools,"* Urban Education (Vol. 22, No. 2, July 1987).

28. Allan F. Abrahamse, Peter A. Morrison, and Linda J. Waite, *Beyond Stereotypes: Who Becomes a Single Teenage Mother?* (Santa Monica, CA: Rand Corporation, 1988).

29. Ibid.

gained by having a baby.[30] If we think of teenage mothers as having the usual adolescent urges to do something meaningful with their lives, then it is not difficult to see why young women lacking the same range of choices as other adolescents are drawn to what is the most revered role for women in our society — motherhood.

Feminist researcher Theresa Cusick pursues this line of reasoning in her analysis of the lure of early parenthood for certain young women:

> Young girls receive the subliminal message that no matter whatever else they aspire to, they will become mothers. And because most teen women expect to become mothers it is not surprising that some impatient teens may choose to become mothers earlier rather than later.

She concludes that young women who start childbearing during their teen-age years "may see motherhood as an honorable escape from a race they cannot win."[31]

Cusick's observations appear to be especially applicable to black teen-age girls who are not college-bound, a group whose prospects for marriage and work have worsened over the past 15 years.[32] Considering that nearly half of these young women have a baby before they are 20, it seems rea-sonable to ask whether their decisions about childbearing are a direct con-sequence of their expectations for the future.[33] Several researchers have concluded that the benefits are indeed small for young black women who defer childbearing.[34] This conclusion appears to confirm the theory that

---

30. Joy Dryfoos, "A Time for New Thinking About Adolescent Pregnancy," *American Journal of Public Health* (Vol. 75, No. 1, 1985).

    Kristin A. Moore and Richard F. Wertheimer, "Teenage Childbearing and Wel-fare: Preventive and Ameliorative Strategies," *Family Planning Perspective* (Vol. 16, No. 6, Nov./Dec. 1984).

31. Theresa Cusick, "Sexism and Early Parenting: Cause and Effect?" (Washington, DC: Project on Equal Education Rights, National Organization of Women Legal De-fense and Educational Fund, 1988).

32. William T. Grant Foundation Commission, op. cit. (see note 6).

33. Stanley Henshaw at the Alan Guttmacher Institute, New York City, reported in a private conversation (1989) that 37% of black women have a child before they are 20. For non-college-bound black teens, the proportion is surely higher.

34. Frank F. Furstenberg, Jr., "Race Differences in Teenage Sexuality, Pregnancy and Adolescent Childbearing," *Milbank Quarterly* (Vol. 65, Suppl. 2, 1987).

    "Teenage Pregnancy: Economic Irrationality or Logical Choice?" Radcliffe News (Cambridge, MA: Summer 1989).

young mothers assess their "life options" and then judge the "opportunity costs" of having a child to be low.[35]

Marital Status

Increasingly, teen mothers are single. As noted in the introduction, today, more than three-fifths of births to teenagers occur outside of marriage.[36] A number of reasons explain why marriage patterns among teenagers who bear children have changed so drastically.[37] First, more young people are postponing marriage, at least in part, because of changing employment opportunities. For instance, since unemployment and sharp reductions in the earnings of young adults are pronounced in impoverished black neighborhoods, it appears that black women are increasingly single because the pool of marriageable black men is shrinking.[38] Second, as the stigma of unwed parenthood has faded, fewer single women of any age are choosing to compound the problems of parenting with those entailed in a hasty marriage. Thus single-mother families are more common throughout our society.

The marital status of teen mothers is affected not only by their probability of marrying but also by their risk of divorce and their chances for remarriage. Marital instability is common among teens who become mothers and marry. Furthermore, young black mothers are much less likely to marry, to remain married, and, if divorced, to remarry than whites.[39]

These new marriage patterns have important implications, both positive and negative, for the economic situation of young mothers in general, and of young black mothers in particular. On the positive side, we know that single teenage mothers are more successful at staying in school than their married counterparts: since a single young mother is more likely to live at home or with adult relatives, she is also more likely to have the financial support and child care that she needs in order to continue with her edu-

---

35. Dryfoos op. cit. (see note 30); and Moore and Wertheimer, op. cit. (see note 30).
36. Pittman and Adams, op. cit. (see note 2).
37. Andrew Cherlin, "The Weakening Link Between Marriage and the Care of Children," *Family Planning Perspectives* (Vol. 20, No. 6, Nov./Dec. 1988).
38. William J. Wilson, *The Truly Disadvantaged: The Inner City, The Underclass, and Public Policy* (Chicago: University of Chicago Press, 1987).
39. Furstenberg, op. cit. (see note 34).

cation.[40] But compared with women in families with two wage earners, single mothers will find it difficult to support themselves and their children.

Fertility Patterns

Early childbearing has a direct effect on completed family size. Births to teens are more closely spaced than births to older women; although the gap is narrowing, teenage mothers tend to have more children than their peers who delay childbearing.[41] Two-fifths of teenage mothers have a second birth within three years of their first.[42] Many experts believe that teenagers can successfully cope with a first birth if it is not followed by another before the mother is prepared for personal and economic independence. With larger families or narrower intervals between children, teenage mothers are less likely to be successful in school and work. These schooling and work disadvantages, in turn, have negative consequences for the development of their children.

Education

School-Age Mothers

Teenage mothers 17 and younger are typically characterized as school-age, and efforts to increase school attendance among teenage parents usually focus on this group. By contrast, mothers aged 18 or 19 are often considered beyond school-age. However, the majority of all teenage mothers — those who give birth this year and those who had children in other years but are still under 20 — have not completed a regular high school diploma or equivalency degree. Therefore, it seems inappropriate to limit the definition of school-age mother and efforts to increase school attendance to those who are 17 or younger.

Unfortunately, we do not have data that would permit us to pinpoint exactly what proportion of teenage mothers are and are not high school grad-

---

40. Katherine F. Darabi, "A Closer Look at Schooling After the First Birth," *The Journal of School Health* (Mar. 1982).
41. Janet C. Quint, Denise F. Polit, and Cynthia A. Guy, *New Chance: Laying the Groundwork for a New Demonstration to Build Human Capital Among Low-Income Young Mothers* (New York: Manpower Demonstration Research Corporation, 1986).
42. Pittman and Adams, op. cit. (see note 2).

uates; but by synthesizing data on several aspects of this issue, we can conclude that more than half have not completed high school:

- The majority of teenagers giving birth in any one year are not high school
  graduates. This comes from information on birth certificates where almost all states record the number of years of schooling the mother has
  completed. According to the data available on women giving birth in
  1986, 38 percent of 19-year-old mothers, 54 percent of 18-year-old
  mothers, and 84 percent of 17-year-old mothers had not completed 12
  years of schooling.[43]

- The majority of all teenage mothers in 1986 had probably not completed
  high school. Given what we know about the ages of all mothers who
  were teenagers in 1986 — those who gave birth that year and those who
  gave birth in earlier years and were still under 20 — we can make a series
  of assumptions about their graduation patterns.[44] One-third of teenage
  mothers in 1986 were 17 or younger, and we can assume that very few
  of them had graduated. Another one-third were 18 or 19, but had begun
  childbearing when they were younger than 18. Since many of them had
  their first child before completing high school and have had subsequent
  children, we can assume that a large proportion of these mothers also
  were not high school graduates. Finally, the remaining one-third were 18
  or 19 and began childbearing at these ages. Since we know that teenage
  mothers lag behind their nonparenting peers in levels of school achievement, we can assume that some of them had not yet completed high
  school.

Educational and School Status

We know that teenage mothers complete fewer years of schooling and
are less likely to graduate from high school than their peers.[45] Convention-
al wisdom holds that early childbearing causes lower levels of educational
attainment among young mothers. But even if teenager mothers were to
postpone childbearing, the preexisting differences between them and their
nonparenting peers would probably lead to different educational outcomes.[46] Indeed, a common set of factors may predispose some young

43. National Center for Health Statistics, "Advance Report of Final Natality Statistics, 1986," *Monthly Vital Statistics Report*, Table 22 (Washington, DC: U.S. Department of Health and Human Services).
44. Dryfoos, op. cit. (see note 8).
45. Cheryl D. Hayes, *Risking the Future* (Washington, DC: National Academy
Press, 1987).
46. Haggstrom et al., op. cit. (see note 26).

women both to pursue less schooling and to start childbearing at a young age.[47] Thus, an adolescent mother's educational experiences are not simply a consequence of becoming a parent before graduating from high school.

Unfortunately, existing evidence does not allow us to describe fully the nature of these experiences — when and how and why young mothers complete their secondary education or fall behind in their schooling. For instance, as was noted in the previous section, we would like to be able to pinpoint how many teenage mothers are high school graduates and how many are not. Furthermore, among those who are not graduates, we would like to be able to determine how many are enrolled in school and how many are dropouts. However, we do not have this information because such data are not routinely collected and because it is difficult to follow the educational progress of young mothers who may leave and return to school several times or take long periods of time to graduate. Nonetheless, many useful findings can be extracted from the data we do have; and by drawing on the latest research, we can piece together the basic features of young mothers' educational patterns.

This story has positive and negative sides. On the one hand, school enrollment among pregnant and parenting teenagers has increased,[48] the GED has become an important route to high school accreditation for younger teen mothers,[49] and higher proportions of young mothers graduate from high school now than ever did before.[50] Consequently, young mothers have reduced the gap in educational attainment between themselves and their peers who start childbearing at older ages.[51]

On the other hand, the majority of teenage mothers are not high school graduates, and compared with their peers who postpone childbearing,

---

47. Dawn M. Upchurch and James McCarthy, "The Effects of the Timing of a First Birth on High School Completion" (Paper presented at the annual meeting of the Population Association of America, Baltimore, Mar. 30-Apr. 1, 1989).

48. Mott and Maxwell, op. cit. (see note 7).

49. Frank L. Mott and William Marsiglio, "Early Childbearing and Completion of High School," *Family Planning Perspectives* (Vol. 17, No. 5, Sept./Oct. 1985).

50. Dawn M. Upchurch and James McCarthy, "Adolescent Childbearing and High School Completion in the 1980s: Have Things Changed?" (Paper presented at the annual meeting of the American Public Health Association, Boston, Nov. 13-17, 1988).

51. Ibid.

of these women have probably benefited from the additional help that school or community services can offer.

Unfortunately, the ability of young mothers in the first group to remain in school through delivery offers no guarantee that they can proceed without interruption to obtain a high school diploma. One study found that about 40 percent of the students enrolled in school when they gave birth dropped out subsequently.[61] Another found that although younger teen mothers are more likely to stay in school after they give birth, it is difficult for them to remain in school.[62] As young women try to meet their child care obligations while continuing to pursue their coursework, the practical problems facing them might be described as the proverbial straw that breaks the camel's back. Help with these practical problems — assistance with arranging suitable care for their children during the time they are attending classes, for instance — is critical to their being able to simultaneously manage their home and school responsibilities.

This kind of practical assistance is necessary but not sufficient for many of the young women in the second and third groups — dropouts who leave school before or during pregnancy. They are more likely than mothers in the first group to embark upon motherhood with a legacy of alienation toward or failure in school. Thus, the impediments to their graduation are often not only situational, but also educational. If these young women are to be brought back into an education program, they must be convinced that school is a setting in which their efforts will improve their future and those of their children. To encourage their return to school, we need to offer them a greater variety of educational options. Educators and researchers in states that are already developing or operating welfare reform programs targeting teen mothers indicate that many young AFDC recipients, who are required to return to school, resist going back to mainstream classes. They prefer alternative schools that offer a more personalized approach to working with students, work/study opportunities, and nontraditional methods of instruction.[63]

A large portion of the young mothers are in the third group: they dropped

61. Upchurch and McCarthy, op. cit. (see note 47).
62. Darabi, op. cit. (see note 40).
63. Telephone conservations with Diane Colby, Milwaukee Public Schools; Caroline Gaston, New Futures School, Alburquerque; and Rebecca Maynard, Mathematica Policy Research, Princeton, N.J., 1988.

out prior to conception. Since these mothers have been out of school for some time, they are often overlooked. They require a more extensive outreach effort than their counterparts in the first two groups, who are easier to identify and follow because they are more visible to educators and service providers. Locating and advising mothers in the third group is time-consuming and depends upon interagency cooperation.

In reviewing the factors that encourage or discourage school completion among teen mothers, one question is likely to occur: Is an emphasis on school attendance really warranted for young women who are pregnant or who have recently given birth? Like most mothers, many teenage mothers want to be the primary care givers for their babies. In view of the demands that pregnancy and care for young children place on them, and in view of the fact that many of them do eventually complete school, it could be argued that in many cases the best course of action is for them to stay out of school for some time — both during the later months of pregnancy and after they deliver.

However, teenagers are more likely to complete high school if they are in an educational program during pregnancy and after birth. Furthermore, many young mothers who delay acquiring a high school diploma face many of the same problems in becoming economically self-sufficient as mothers who never graduate. Consequently, whatever the difficulties involved, teen mothers should be encouraged to pursue academic coursework and care for their babies simultaneously; but, it is critical that communities help them to do this without compromising their children's well-being.

Prospects for Economic Well-being

A woman who gives birth to her first child as a teenager is more vulnerable to poverty than her peers who delay childbearing; however, if a woman who starts childbearing at an older age comes from a low-income family, is poorly educated, divorces or never marries, and has closely spaced children, chances are good that she, too, will have a low standard of living. Thus, the negative economic consequences associated with teenage parenthood are caused not by the age at childbirth alone, but by a combination of factors both before and after an early birth — such as a young woman's personal, family, and socioeconomic circumstances before she gives

birth and her fertility patterns, marital experiences, and educational ac-
complishments after she becomes a mother.

Other factors also predispose teenage mothers to economic instability,
but they are frequently overlooked. This was especially obvious in the in-
tense public debate that took place over the last decade about teenage
mothers' use of welfare. Many commentators attributed young mothers' re-
liance on welfare to their childbirth decisions and to deficits in themselves,
their families, and their neighborhoods. Few made reference to deficien-
cies in the ways in which schools and other youth-serving institutions have
traditionally prepared young women for employment and in the support
available to working mothers.

A more realistic assessment of the economic problems of teenage mothers would take into account that many mothers with limited educational
credentials cannot support themselves; expenditures on child care alone
account for nearly one-third of poor mothers' income.[64] Other mothers
conclude that full-time employment is not worth the stress it places on their
family life. When a mother considers the difficulties involved in locating
affordable and appropriate child care, and in transporting herself and her
child back and forth from work, and when she also considers the arrangements that she must make if her child or the care giver is sick, she may well
decide that both she and her family will be better served if she does not
work full-time. (A large proportion of American mothers have apparently
come to this conclusion: only 44 percent of mothers with dependent children have full-time jobs.[65])

Given the options for economic support that are available to mothers,
it is not surprising, as two researchers have concluded, that welfare gives
women who begin childbearing as teenagers an "unavoidable if unattrac-
tive alternative to paid employment."[66] A large proportion of young mothers will rely on public assistance at some point in time.[67] While most of

---

64. Mathematica Policy Research, "The Child Care Challenge: What Parents Need
and What is Available in Three Metropolitan Areas," (Princeton, NJ: 1989).
65. Arlie Hochschild, *The Second Shift: Working Parents and the Revolution at
Home* (New York: Viking, 1989).
   David Ellwood, *Targeting Would-be Long-term Recipients of AFDC* (Princeton,
NJ: Mathematica Policy Research, 1986).
66. Moore and Wertheimer, op. cit. (see note 30).
67. Dianne S. Burden and Lorraine V. Klerman, "Teenage Parenthood: Factors That
Lessen Economic Dependence," *Social Work* (Jan.-Feb. 1984).

these mothers use welfare only for temporary help, a significant minority rely on it for 8 to 10 years, or more.[68]

Nevertheless, young mothers are highly motivated to work. Almost all interviews with young mothers show that they want to support themselves and that they recognize that improvements in their family's well-being will depend on their working. In fact, giving birth during adolescence does not reduce the amount of time a woman will participate in the labor force over her lifetime.[69]

*   *   *

In a recent literature review, the authors noted that teenage mothers need not be "doomed by an early birth":

> If a successful intervention can be launched to assist them in completing their educations and controlling their fertility, many of the debilitating conditions associated with early childbearing can presumably be averted.[70]

Interventions for teenage mothers can be organized in a variety of institutional settings. Nonetheless, there is reason to recommend that school districts take the lead role in orchestrating educational interventions for pregnant and parenting students. If one of the primary goals of these interventions is to help teens complete their schooling and acquire basic education skills, then the educational system must be centrally involved in such efforts. Schools are also a natural base for programs for this population because they are in contact with more adolescents than any other institution in the community. However, schools must collaborate with other groups and agencies in order to provide a comprehensive array of services. For instance, the vast majority of mothers-to-be and mothers who are not high school graduates drop out of school for some period of time, and schools must rely upon interagency cooperation in locating and helping them. The next chapter describes what schools have done so far to help pregnant and parenting students stay enrolled and then presents information on promising approaches for improving educational support for these students.

---

68. Furstenberg et al., op. cit. (see note 55).
69. Quint, et. al., op. cit. (see note 41).
70. Ibid.

CHAPTER TWO

SCHOOLS AND STUDENT PARENTHOOD

This chapter summarizes the research on how schools and school districts have responded to students who are pregnant or mothers. It also describes some recent initiatives to expand the types of assistance offered to these students.

Traditionally, coping with adolescent parenthood was regarded as the responsibility of the family, not of the school. Usually, health and social service agencies provided whatever help was available for young mothers. Often these services were directed exclusively to unmarried mothers, and most programs focused on pregnancy and the immediate postpartum period. With a few exceptions, the educational needs of pregnant and parenting students were not taken seriously until Title IX of the Education Amendments of 1972 went into effect and a greater number of public grants for serving this population were made available to schools. Then, some schools received federal funding through the Office of Adolescent Pregnancy Programs and the Maternal and Child Health program; in a few states — for example, California — state funds supported school-based programs for pregnant and parenting students.[71]

With this additional support, more school districts established programs for pregnant girls and young mothers in their own facilities during the late 1970s. A 1979 1980 study of 127 cities in the United States revealed that 90 had at least one program for pregnant or parenting students, 83 of which were sponsored by local school districts.[72] However, none of these pro-

71. Helen H. Cagampang, William H. Gerritz, and Gerald C. Hayward, *Pregnant and Parenting Minors in California Schools* (Berkeley: School of Education, University of California, 1987).
72. Asta M. Kenney, "Teen Pregnancy: An Issue for Schools," *Phi Delta Kappa* (June 1987).

grams was comprehensive, and most would not have been established without the hard work of a few highly committed educators, or sometimes local service providers, who lobbied school administrators to do more for these students.[73]

The Role of Comprehensive Programs

Over the last decade, programs for pregnant and parenting teens, and sometimes for their children, have become more common.[74] Many of these programs are connected to school systems, but often they operate with a degree of autonomy — for example, in buildings other than the regular school sites or as schools-within-schools. They usually aim to be comprehensive — to include the range of services teenage mothers need in order to continue school, delay having a second child, prepare realistically for work, and provide adequately for their children. Therefore, the programs try to offer students a mix of services — education, personal guidance, health, and occasionally job training and placement — that are engaging, tailored to their needs, and respectful of their strengths. Typically, their staff members also assist young mothers in negotiating with other public and community service providers.

Many of these programs have well-deserved reputations for excellence and have served as models for other initiatives.[75] While funds for rigorous evaluation have been limited, existing evidence suggests that those that are carefully designed and skillfully operated by compassionate, nurturing staff have a positive impact on young mothers.[76]

These programs, however, are not without their problems. One drawback is that many do not sufficiently emphasize school completion. Another shortcoming is that most are not able to offer the array of services that

73. Gail Zellman, *The Response of the Schools to Teenage Pregnancy and Parenthood* (Santa Monica, CA: Rand Corporation, 1981).

74. Judith Francis and Fern Marx, *Learning Together: A National Directory of Teen Parenting and Child Care Programs* (Wellesley, MA: Center for Research on Women, Wellesley College, 1989).

75. Phyllis Smith Nickel and Holly Delany, *Working with Teen Parents: A Survey of Promising Approaches* (Chicago: Family Resource Coalition, 1985).

76. Anita M. Mitchell and Debra K. Walker, "Impact Evaluation of Too Early Childbearing Programs," final report of Southwest Regional Laboratories to the Charles Stewart Mott Foundation, Los Alamitos, 1985.

would make them truly comprehensive.[77] Staff then have to rely on referrals to other agencies, and often the teen participant simply cannot manage making the arrangements required to get help from multiple service providers. What is more, she loses time in school while she seeks these services.

Special programs need strengthening in several other areas as well. Because they wish to avoid controversy, a number of programs offer teenagers very limited family planning education and counseling. Yet effective assistance with family planning, including education, personal guidance, and medical services, is critical to helping teenage mothers postpone additional births. Also, most programs do not adequately prepare teens for employment; and programs that work with the children of teenage parents typically serve only a small number of children.[78] One final limitation of these programs is that the quality of the educational component varies enormously. Some programs have developed innovative approaches to helping students keep up with their schoolwork and are creative in drawing upon students' experiences with pregnancy and parenthood as a means of engaging them in learning, but others offer only minimal opportunities for academic growth.

However serious, these problems do not in any way call into question the usefulness of special programs for teen mothers. However, additional limitations associated with these programs suggest that they ought to be regarded as only *one component* of a broader community plan to assist pregnant and parenting teens, not — as is too often the case — as the focus of most or all of a school district's or a community's efforts on behalf of this population.

A major limitation is that the programs usually rely on informal methods of identifying pregnant and parenting students who dropped out of school before conception, during pregnancy, or after giving birth. Another shortcoming is that the programs are far more likely to concentrate on pregnant than on parenting teens.[79] For example, the California Department of Education administers two legally mandated school-based programs, one for

---

77. Richard A. Weatherley, Sylvia B. Perlman, Michael Levine, and Lorraine Klerman. *Patchwork Programs: Comprehensive Services for Pregnant and Parenting Adolescents* (Seattle: Center for Social Welfare Research, School of Social Work, University of Washington, 1985).

78. Francis and Marx, op. cit. (see note 74).

79. Support Center for Educational Equity for Young Mothers, op. cit. (see note 13).

pregnant and the other for parenting teens. While the Pregnant Minor Program operates in 119 sites, the School-age Parent and Infant Development Program is in only 49 sites.[80] Yet teen parents who need to complete high school outnumber pregnant teens who have not yet graduated.

A related problem is that special programs tend to take a "crisis intervention" approach; few work with teens for a long period of time.[81] The program's policies require that at some point after students give birth — whether after six weeks, after six months, or at the end of the semester in which they deliver — they return to their home schools. The schools, however, typically make no provision for offering them special help — for example, with their child care responsibilities. Not surprisingly, many of these mothers drop out of school and out of the network of services available to teen parents, making it all the more likely that they will have additional children in rapid succession.

One reason young mothers experience such an abrupt change when they return to their regular school is that the special programs are usually not integrated into a *continuum of services* for pregnant and parenting students. A Rand Corporation study on the responses of schools to teenage pregnancy describes how staff at regular schools use special programs for pregnant teens:

> The regular school acts as though the student is leaving permanently. As with other types of transfer, all her records are sent to the program and she is dropped from her counselor's caseload. . . . Whether she reenters is thus not that school's business. On the informal level, plans for regular school return are seldom discussed. Rarely does a counselor suggest that a student call and keep in touch. The opportunity to build in an expectation of regular school return is simply not seized . . . the school's limited policies surrounding pregnancy-related activities come to an end at the point at which enrollment in the special program is recommended; few policies or procedures exist for working with a pregnant student past this point in a pregnancy.[82]

What all these patterns suggest is that school-based interventions for young mothers are too brief: they rarely extend beyond a semester or, at most, a year. A study of one comprehensive although relatively short-term service program for young, low-income pregnant and parenting teens

---

80. Brindis and Jeremy, op. cit. (see note 12).
81. Weatherley et al., op. cit. (see note 77).
82. Zellman, op. cit. (see note 73).

found that it improved educational outcomes, but that many of the effects were only temporary.[83] In other words, if interventions are not sustained, much of the investment that the special programs have made in helping teen mothers will be lost.

Mainstream Schools

As the preceding observations suggest, in order to assess how well communities have handled the educational problems of pregnant and parenting teenagers, we must consider not only their special programs but also the broader policies, practices, and programs of regular schools and the school district. The need to do so becomes especially apparent when we recognize that in addition to their tendency to enroll teens for relatively brief time spans, special programs reach only a fraction of the population that needs services. For example, California's two legally mandated programs for pregnant and parenting students serve fewer than 12 percent of those who are eligible.[84]

The Rand study discussed in the previous section found that staff at regular schools do not use special programs appropriately. This finding is but one of many that led the researchers to conclude that the schools they studied usually adopted a passive stance to the problems of pregnant and parenting teenagers. Administrators construed the mandate of Title IX narrowly by holding themselves responsible only for *not* excluding pregnant or parenting students. The researchers offered this summary of their investigations:

> Student pregnancy and parenthood are rarely discussed in the 30 regular schools we visited; few schools have comprehensive policies designed to help students maintain school attendance. . . . Pregnancy resolution decisions and dropout decisions are almost always left to pregnant students and their families.

The researchers made a number of observations to substantiate their conclusion that "schools neither seek nor want an active role in student pregnancy and parenthood." For instance, they noted "Little time and few

83. Denise F. Polit, Janet C. Quint, and James Riccio, *The Challenge of Serving Teenage Mothers: Lessons from Project Redirection* (New York: Manpower Demonstration Research Corporation, 1988).
84. Brindis and Jeremy, op. cit. (see note 12).

resources are devoted to increasing regular school staff awareness of student pregnancy and parenthood. We saw no case in which the principal had used her or his position to make the issue salient." Principals "reinforced the views of many regular program staff that student pregnancy and parenthood should be ignored, if possible."

The Rand study demonstrated that one result of this lack of leadership was that staff members' views about adolescent pregnancy dominated the school, because "when policies are informal and casually enforced, attitudes dictate policy." Not surprisingly, given their many other responsibilities, staff members often hesitated to involve themselves in the problems of pregnant and parenting students, and the needs of these students thus were often overlooked. Moreover, the researchers suggested, "staff attitudes plus lack of active support and clear policy" in the regular schools were a signal to pregnant and parenting students that they should consider their problems personal and resolve them on their own. The researchers reasoned that without active encouragement, such students might be "reluctant to risk exposure to negative attitudes by contacting staff members or officially involving the school in their situation."

A recent study presented a similar critique of how schools respond to pregnant students and young mothers. The authors of this study noted:

> What the girls whom we interviewed made clear to us . . . was that the staffs of Chicago public schools they attended paid little attention to the needs of pregnant and parenting teens. In fact, it appeared that only girls who had made good friends with a teacher, or more rarely a counselor or member of the administration, were likely to get much assistance at their school, unless they transferred to one of the three schools for pregnant teens. However, even then, they were likely to become invisible again when they re-enrolled in their home school. There were reports of helpful teachers and staff. Individually, school employees provided support and help. But the record was more one of inconsistent assistance and invisibility.[85]

Another recent report based on a survey of 12 diverse schools across the country cited many instances of inequitable treatment of pregnant and parenting students and concluded that the response to these students is generally not in compliance with Title IX of the Education Amendments of

85. G. Alfred Hess, Denise O'Neil Green, Elliot Stapleton, and Olga Reyes, *Invisibly Pregnant: Teenage Mothers in the Chicago Press Schools* (Chicago: Chicago Panel on Public School Policy and Finance, 1988).

1972, the law that prohibits sex discrimination in schools receiving federal funds.[86]

District Policies

School district policies toward students who are pregnant or mothers appear to mirror the problems of the individual schools. The findings of a 1988 survey conducted by the Academy for Educational Development (AED) on policies, practices, programs, and plans for pregnant and parenting students in nine urban school districts include the following:

- *Administrators often lack important information about the pregnant and parenting teens in their districts.* Administrators' knowledge of this group of students is uneven. While many administrators know their cities' annual rate of births to teen mothers, most do not know the number of pregnant and parenting teenagers in their districts, what proportion of these teenagers had not compleüted high school, and what proportion of female dropouts in their districts are mothers.

- *Support for young mothers is more limited than is support for pregnant girls.* When school systems set up special programs in response to teenage parenthood, these programs usually serve pregnant students. If special services for student mothers are established, most of them target a small number of students.

- *Assistance for pregnant and parenting students is usually organized as innovations in service delivery rather than as improvements in institutional policies.* Typically, help for pregnant and parenting students is provided through special programs and services. Most districts have not pursued broader policy reforms that would encourage this group of students to remain in or return to school, such as flexible scheduling and a shorter school day.

- *Dropouts are shortchanged in programs established to respond to student parenthood.* Most administrators concerned about pregnant girls and teenage mothers focus on those who are still in school. Outreach mechanisms to locate and re-enroll dropouts who are parents or are about to become parents are weak.

- *Dropout prevention initiatives slight the needs of pregnant and parenting students.* Dropout prevention and other at-risk youth initiatives often cite teenage pregnancy as an issue, but infrequently allocate funds for improving assistance to pregnant and parenting students.

---

86. Nash and Dunkle, op. cit. (see note 10).

33

- *Coordination among public-sector agencies working with teenage mothers is limited.* There is little formal collaboration among staff of welfare, health, social service, and education agencies in terms of identifying and serving school-age mothers who have not completed high school.

- *When administrators develop new plans for improving help to pregnant and parenting students, their scope is often limited.* Administrators have many ideas for helping pregnant and parenting teenagers more effectively. Few, however, focus on significant changes in school policies, on efforts to coordinate the services of a number of different program operators, or on a comprehensive approach.[87]

It is necessary to view these findings in their proper context. In AED's report on this survey, entitled *Improving Educational Opportunities for Pregnant and Parenting Students*, the authors suggest that while many dedicated individuals are working to help young mothers-to-be and mothers, a number of factors explain why school administrators do not pay enough attention to the problems of these young women. Pregnant and parenting teens are disproportionately poor, minority, and behind grade level in school. They are sometimes seen as irresponsible for having had sex and children. Also, they are frequently out of sight and therefore out of mind: they either have left school or have enrolled in a special program that keeps them away from the mainstream schools. Finally, they have needs — for instance, for work/study options, child care, and flexible scheduling — that many educational institutions are not now equipped to meet.

Moreover, the authors note, contemporary schools have been given a mission that their predecessors were never held to — educating all adolescents. While it was once considered an individual student's responsibility to become educated, the schools have now been charged with the task of making certain that the student completes school. It is exceedingly difficult, especially in an era of fiscal constraints, for schools to adjust to this change, and it is therefore not surprising that they overlook the problems of pregnant and parenting teens.

The report's analysis of the survey findings ends with these observations:

> Thus, while we found both lack of knowledge and stereotyping to be major factors in why the educational needs of pregnant and parenting teens are inadequately addressed, we were more impressed with administrators' sense of being overwhelmed. Administrators lack the critical ingredients that facil-

---

87. Support Center for Educational Equity for Young Mothers, op. cit. (see note 13).

itate change: solid *knowledge* about the numbers of pregnant and parenting teens; *leadership,* because school personnel with extensive knowledge of this population are typically not included in planning groups focusing on school improvement and dropout prevention; *models,* because very few districts have tried to make systemic changes on behalf of this population; and, as many survey respondents noted, *resources* for approaches they see as appropriate but expensive — school-based child care and case managers, for instance.

Furthermore, in many places, administrators still fear opposition if they try to help these students more adequately. Without a vision of what should be done, solid information about how to make appropriate change, and monetary incentives to pursue improvements, administrators are naturally reluctant to extend themselves to a controversial group of students.

The authors conclude that while modest progress has been made in improving educational opportunities for pregnant and parenting students, most school districts offer these young women a patchwork of programs and regulations rather than a sustained and comprehensive approach to helping them complete their education.

Directions for Change

In order to increase the proportion of teenage mothers who complete their secondary education and do so without lagging very far behind their nonparenting peers, staff in schools and school districts must hold themselves accountable for the educational progress of pregnant and parenting teenagers who are not high school graduates. While special programs for pregnant girls and young mothers are invaluable if they are of high quality, they should be part of a continuum of care. Thus, educational administrators and practitioners will have to develop a broad array of academic options and support services that will make it easier for these students to succeed. And they must attend to the policies, programs, and practices in their school districts and in individual schools that adversely affect these students or provide insufficient support for them.

Unfortunately, few communities are pursuing full-scale efforts to improve young mothers' chances of graduating from high school. Nonetheless, a number of initiatives provide examples of the types of changes that are needed to expand the support districts offer pregnant and parenting students through their traditional programs for this population. Three initiatives are described briefly here — a school-based program offering counseling and advocacy, sponsored by the National State Boards of Education (NASBE); a school-centered service coordination strategy launched by the New York City Dropout Prevention Program; and a case-management model, the Teenage Pregnancy and Parenting Program (TAPP) in San Francisco. (See the Appendix for information on how to contact the sponsoring agencies.)

The NASBE demonstration operates in two high schools.[88] A counselor/advocate is responsible for overseeing efforts to help the pregnant and parenting students in each school. The counselor serves as a case manager, referring teens to needed health and social services in the community, tracking their attendance and academic progress, and informing them about various educational programs. In addition, she or he acts as a personal counselor to the students. To support this work, the program gives the teens access to a parenting class and the services of a school nurse. A committee composed of representatives from the school system and from health, social services, and community-based organizations meets regularly to guide the program and help the counselor/advocate get access to the services the teens need.

Preliminary results from the program suggest that it has been successful in a range of areas. They include building a network of service referrals to help teens stay in school, apprising them of their academic options, promoting districtwide coordination of efforts to help pregnant and parenting teens, involving teen fathers and parents of teen mothers in program activities, and maintaining program visibility.

The Dropout Prevention Program of the Board of Education of the City of New York has developed a similar approach to the one used in the NASBE project. Called the Services Linkages Project for Parenting Adolescents, it is a service coordination and improvement project that was launched initially in nine schools and will expand soon to include many more sites.[89] In each school, staff members serving as "school designates for teen pregnancy" work with both pregnant and parenting students to

88. Janice Earle and Marie Schumacher, "Counselor/Advocates: Keeping Pregnant and Parenting Teens in School" (Alexandria, VA: National Association of State Boards of Education, 1988).
89. Juliet Ucelli, "The Services Linkage Project for Parenting Adolescents" (New York: Dropout Prevention Program, Board of Education of the City of New York, 1988).

help them get access to services, and with other staff to encourage them to be more responsive to these students. Because their work is complex, encompassing both individual counseling and efforts to effect institutional change, the school designates receive support and training from a social worker in the Dropout Prevention Program's central office.

San Francisco's TAPP operates citywide.[90] In existence since 1981, the program is coordinated by the San Francisco Unified School District and the Family Service Agency of San Francisco. The Department of Social Services and the Department of Public Health are key participants among the 30 service agencies that oversee the program. TAPP combines case-management services with an advocacy approach for improving the responsiveness of public institutions to pregnant and parenting teenagers. The teenagers who use TAPP are assigned to a "continuous counselor," who follows 30-40 students and assists them in securing services that are specified in their individualized case plans. Through its monitoring and other data systems, the program has been able to document that school retention and re-enrollment rates among its participants exceed the national average.

Using these kinds of innovations to develop a more systematic approach to helping pregnant and parenting teenagers complete high school is a significant challenge. How to meet that challenge is the subject of the next chapter.

---

90. Claire Brindis, Richard P. Barth, and Amy B. Loomis, "Continuous Counseling: Case Management with Teenage Parents," *Social Casework* (Mar. 1987).

CHAPTER THREE

MAKING CHANGE

This chapter describes how to organize a community-level effort to improve school policies, programs, and practices for young mothers who are not high school graduates. It includes guidelines for forming a collaborative advisory group and using this group to gather information on the educational needs of pregnant and parenting students in the community, to develop recommendations for addressing these needs, and to advocate for change.

Organizing a Collaborative Advisory Group

In an era of fiscal constraints, reducing the obstacles to school enrollment and completion among young mothers-to-be and mothers will require new types of cooperation among the public and private agencies in a community. To lay the groundwork for reforms, a collaborative advisory group should convene to formulate policy recommendations for the school system. One expert on adolescent pregnancy issues describes what such groups can accomplish:

> These groups can create change on two important levels. First, by knowing the staff members and programs, the group can work out informal solutions for problems of individual students. Second, by having the "big picture" of services provided to this population, the committee can identify. . . structural or formal problems and barriers.[91]

---

91. Margaret Dunkle, *Promoting Collaboration, Promoting Success: Educators Working with Communities on Teenage Pregnancy and Parenting* (Washington, DC: Equality Center, 1989).

See also Jeanne Lindsay and Sharon Rodine, *Teen Pregnancy Challenge: Strategies for Change* and *Teen Pregnancy Challenge: Programs For Kids* (Buena Park, CA: Morning Glory Press, 1989), for tips on organizing community coalitions.

A recent New York City experience illustrates the power of an advisory group to create the momentum for change within a school district. In 1988 the city's Board of Education selected a new chancellor. A group of activists immediately recognized that this appointment was an opportunity to press for fresh attention to the needs of pregnant girls and young parents. They arranged to meet with members of the chancellor's transition team, contacted one of his assistants known for his commitment to improving services to young parents, and met monthly in order to draft an advocacy statement, entitled *A Call to Action*, that was directed to the chancellor and his staff. In response to these efforts, the chancellor appointed the Working Group on Educational Opportunities for Pregnant and Parenting Adolescents.

Cochaired by a member of the chancellor's staff and a leading teenage pregnancy expert from an advocacy organization specializing in the problems of low-income women and girls, the Working Group included 35 high-level representatives of departments in the school system, other public agencies, and private youth-serving organizations. They joined teenage pregnancy activists for a series of meetings in order to develop recommendations for the chancellor. In their last meeting, members of the Working Group gave their approval to a report presenting these recommendations, *Helping Pregnant and Parenting Students Complete High School in New York City: Recommendations of the Chancellor's Working Group on Educational Opportunities for Pregnant and Parenting Adolescents.* (See the Appendix for information on how to obtain three documents related to the formation and findings of the Working Group.)

From the outset, membership in the New York City group included many educators and a good cross section of school system staff members who would be responsible for putting most of the proposed changes into practice. But membership also extended beyond educators, thus facilitating interagency coordination and planning. Any such group ought to draw on the knowledge and experience of staff members from the school system and a wide range of organizations outside the schools. As one activist has observed:

> The inside-outside nature of this type of collaboration is critical. You need the outside people — people from the community — to generate public concern. But you can't paste on change from the outside. The inside people — the school people — need to be deeply involved in the deliberations so that

they are committed to pursuing whatever changes the group ultimately recommends.[92]

At a minimum, such an advisory group should include experts and activists from the following types of groups:

- the school system — the superintendent's office, junior and senior high schools, special programs for pregnant students or student mothers, alternative schools serving a significant number of teenage parents, pupil personnel services (guidance counselors, psychologists or social workers, and school nurses), and dropout prevention or at-risk youth initiatives;

- community-based service providers with youth programs that assist pregnant or parenting teens and agencies concerned about teenage parenthood;

- health facilities — for example, adolescent maternity programs, family planning programs, and the Visiting Nurses Association;

- relevant neighborhood institutions — including churches and grass-roots organizations; and

- the welfare department.

Involving representatives of the welfare department, an agency typically unaccustomed to working with the school system, is particularly important. Already in several states, experiments are under way that require minor parents on the welfare rolls to attend high school or work toward a GED as a condition of receiving public assistance. The national welfare reform legislation of 1988 is intended to extend this system nationwide; and if state legislatures are willing to match federal funds, states can obtain federal assistance for supportive services that teens are likely to need to continue in school — child care and possibly other kinds of help. This legislation — sometimes referred to as learnfare — is controversial. Nonetheless, it offers communities an opportunity to develop more effective approaches to educating dropouts. Furthermore, involving welfare administrators in an advisory group should increase the likelihood that educational initiatives targeting young welfare mothers will result in sound educational experiences for them.

---

92. Lisa Syron, Center for Public Advocacy Research, New York, telephone conversation, 1989.

As the advisory group assembles, the members should be certain that they have the authority to recommend significant changes in the methods their agencies use to serve pregnant and parenting teenagers. This principle applies to all agencies represented on the advisory group, but particularly to the school system. Unless the group has received assurances from district administrators that they will seriously entertain ideas for changes in school policies and practices, its first task should be to try to secure such a commitment. Once it has done so, the group is ready to proceed.

Handling Controversy

As the advisory group convenes, it is possible that it will encounter opposition. A decision to bring together representatives of community groups to try to strengthen assistance for young mothers can be a controversial step. There may be people in the community who believe that helping young mothers encourages adolescent pregnancy and diverts scarce resources away from more "deserving" at-risk students. Even if the group does not initially encounter opposition, some group members may be concerned about the potential for it to erupt; they may simply fear the prospect of divisive disagreements, or they may hesitate to involve themselves further in a group that could become immobilized by conflict.

In order to reassure group members that an advisory group can handle controversy, consider the advice of one advocate who looks upon controversy as an opportunity rather than a crisis:

> Make controversy your ally! Make it work for you. When you have people's attention it is easier to identify those who favor change and are willing to work hard to make things better. It is also easier to mobilize the moderates because in the course of discussing the issues involved often they realize they don't want to be part of keeping things as they are. As for the opposition, when they are included in a group that welcomes all viewpoints, where differences can be aired and compromises forged, then it is easier for them to join you in trying to develop approaches that have broad support. Even if this doesn't occur, they are more likely to soften their opposition.[93]

Also, capitalize on the fact that while the needs of adolescent parents may be a controversial topic for the community, similar needs among other

---

93. Constancia Warren, Center for Public Advocacy Research, New York, telephone conversation, 1989.

students are probably more familiar and less divisive. Thus, it may be helpful to place the group's mission in a larger context. An education activist who works on adolescent pregnancy problems reports:

> We were able to mobilize a good deal of support for our efforts by describing our concerns in terms that many people could hook on to. We talked about the problems of student mothers in terms of sex equity; dropout prevention; new approaches for students with adult responsibilities; and the needs of the children of teenage mothers, who are the city's next generation of students.[94]

Furthermore, remember that the type of group that has assembled will itself help to defuse controversy. The fact that the group will be broadly representative of interested agencies and groups and has carefully chosen leaders will strengthen the chances that the members can overcome disagreements and develop recommendations that will be realistic and well received. In addition, the group can proceed with some confidence that the actual *process* the group will follow should help to head off controversy. As the group works together, members ought to have ample opportunity to air their differences. Thus, group meetings should serve as a testing and training ground for the later work of bringing the recommendations before the community. Given this important function, the leaders must help members build their consensus deliberately and have patience with the time required to negotiate compromises. The education activist just cited cautions, "Working out your recommendations is a laborious process; you have to get people to buy in at every step."[95]

If the group is still haunted by the fear that it may spend a lot of time trying to resolve disagreements, remember that the group always has the option of walking away from a tough issue for a while and turning its attention to a less-difficult one. In other words, try to think strategically, and avoid becoming so bogged down by one particular conflict that you lose sight of your overall goals.

One last word about controversy: If the group encounters strong opposition to even forming an advisory group, one tactic is to assemble a fact-finding body rather than an advisory group. The fact-finding group's mission will be to find out more about the educational needs of teen mothers

---

94. Lisa Syron (Speech presented at the Urban Dropout-Prevention Collaboratives Conference, New York, Academy for Educational Development, May 23, 1989).
95. Syron, op. cit. (see note 92).

in the community, and proceed with the work of information gathering described in the next section. When that group has the information it needs, it can come forward with a clear analysis of why the community ought to have an advisory group that can tackle the work of developing recommendations as outlined later in this chapter.

Getting Started

Think of the group's work as falling into two phases. In the first phase, the group should supplement the national information available in the previous two chapters with local information on pregnant and parenting teens and the school system's response to them. In the second phase, the group should lay out the basic features of a comprehensive plan for improving educational opportunities for pregnant and parenting teenagers, draw up recommendations based on this plan, produce a report that presents these recommendations to the groups in the community with a potential interest in the well-being of teenage mothers and their families, and develop an advocacy strategy for acting on these recommendations.

It is a long and cumbersome process to gather information, conceptualize a plan for improved service delivery, formulate recommendations, develop a report, and advocate for change. This process is time-consuming. Try to secure a small grant from a private foundation or corporate donor to support your work. (The work of writing the final report for the New York City Working Group, described earlier, was supported by a foundation grant.)

Group members will have to organize themselves carefully in order to manage a range of complex activities. The group will need a formal leadership structure; and to ensure that recommendations are taken seriously, group members must think very strategically about the constituencies those leaders represent. The group will be best served by having cochairs, one from inside and one from outside the school system. These leaders must have a number of skills and resources: knowledge about the problems of young mothers, access to those who have the power to effect change, competence in facilitating group discussions, strong interpersonal skills, and time to devote to this project. Appointing cochairs improves the chances that your leaders will bring many of these qualities to the group.

The group will also need to identify someone who can take charge of organizing the information gathered and later of drafting recommendations and a report. This person should have strong writing skills. The writer also must have tact — for meeting with group members and others, both individually and in small groups, to discuss the language as well as the substance of the report and of other preliminary documents the group produces as the basis for the final report.

In developing a schedule for the group, plan for monthly meetings. Between meetings, the cochairs, report writer, and committees, if the group has them, can hold smaller meetings or telephone consultations as needed.

To launch the group's work together, devote a meeting to an initial examination of how well the educational needs of teen mothers in your community are being met. The education activist previously quoted stresses the importance of setting aside time for this sort of exercise in one of the group's first meetings:

> Group members come to a planning group with a general appreciation of the problem, but their grasp of the issues is somewhat abstract and removed. They will be more effective if the problem really engages them in a way that makes them personally want to solve it.[96]

In order to help group members focus on the problems facing typical pregnant students and young mothers in the community, develop brief profiles of a few such students or use the profiles in the preface to this book. Divide the group into smaller groups and discuss the profiles, concentrating on the educational needs of the students described. Once the smaller groups have identified these needs, members should go on to ask themselves how well community agencies — schools and other youth-serving institutions — are meeting these needs. In the last 20 minutes of the meeting, pull the larger group back together and review the ideas and conclusions expressed in the small groups.

Gathering Information

Having sharpened members' mental images of the kinds of students the group is trying to help and the types of assistance currently offered to them, the group is now ready to take a closer look at these students and the assistance available to them in the community. Use the *student review* (see Figure 1) to obtain more information about pregnant and parenting teen-

---

96. Ibid.

FIGURE 1

STUDENT REVIEW

In order to develop a deeper understanding of the numbers and educational needs of the young mothers-to-be and mothers in the community, consider these questions:

1. How many pregnant teenagers (who are going to term) and teenage mothers live in the community?

2. What proportion of these pregnant girls and young mothers have not completed high school?

3. Among pregnant teens and teen mothers who do not have a high school diploma, what proportion are pursuing their education either through the school system or through a GED program?

4. What proportion of pregnant students and young mothers without a high school diploma need academic course work that is not at the high school level (middle-school-level course work or other specialized educational services)?

These are hard questions. The group may have to settle for guesstimates based on partial data. Or it may decide that devoting a great deal of time to these questions is not helpful at this point. If so, concentrate on getting some basic information and then try to determine whether the educational patterns and needs of pregnant and parenting teens in the community differ from national trends. If the group wants to explore these questions in some detail, the Appendix provides guidelines that will help the group obtain more information.

agers who have not completed high school and use the *service review* (see Figure 2) to learn more about the support your school system offers these teens.

In order to work on the student and service reviews, the group should divide in two. Half of the group should investigate the questions posed in the student review and the other half should investigate questions posed in the service review. The group may want to divide each of these sub-groups into smaller committees that can take responsibility for one or two of the questions found in these reviews. While the committees are involved in this fact-finding work, cancel the monthly meeting of the overall advisory group. Reconvene when the committees are ready to report their findings. After the group has reviewed these reports, devote at least one meeting to an assessment of this information.

As group members discuss what is happening in the school district and begin to assess how much is being done to meet the educational needs of pregnant and parenting students, often it is easier to focus on the shortcomings in current approaches — the availability of assistance or inadequacy of services. For example, the district may make no provision for monitoring whether a young mother who is returning to her home school after having spent time at a school for pregnant girls manages to stay enrolled in the mainstream school. Or the few school-based child care facilities that exist may not do enough to help young mothers learn about child development. However, it is also essential to focus on the strengths of the district, because the group's recommendations should try to build upon and expand what the district does well.

An assessment of how pregnant and parenting students are faring in the school system should be followed by a discussion of what a more effective approach to helping pregnant and parenting teens with their schooling would look like. For each of the questions included in the complete service review (in the Appendix), try to specify what types of change ought to take place. Developing sound policies in each of these areas should give you the fundamental features of a comprehensive plan to improve educational opportunities for young mothers and mothers-to-be in your community. Now the group is ready to move into the second phase and develop recommendations for reducing the gap between what is happening and what group members think ought to be done.

FIGURE 2

SERVICE REVIEW

The group should gather as much information as needed to answer the following questions about the policies, programs, and practices of the local school district. The Appendix offers a more extensive list of questions to guide the group's investigations.

1. What are the school district policies, programs, and practices that are explicitly directed to pregnant and parenting students?

2. What policies, programs, and practices of the school system that are not explicitly aimed at pregnant and parenting teenagers nevertheless have significant effects on their educational experiences?

3. How do staff members treat pregnant and parenting students?

4. What efforts are being made in the district to ensure that the children of teenage mothers will be adequately prepared to enter school?

5. What are the strengths and shortcomings of the school district's policies, programs, and practices just reviewed?

Developing Recommendations

As the group embarks on the difficult task of developing recommendations, it is likely to find more problems than the members can discuss in a reasonable period of time — for example, within six months. If that is the case, the group will probably want to develop a list of issues that can be addressed in some detail in the recommendations, and a list of issues that cannot be covered in depth. For this second list, the group can provide broad guidelines for others who will address them. For example, while it is critical that community health care facilities and schools work cooperatively to identify young mothers who are out of school, group members may believe that these institutions must develop the specific ways they will carry out this work. Therefore, the group may conclude that in its recommendations it will only highlight the need for change in this area.

Faced with choices about where to focus its energies first, each group will make different decisions, depending on the values and beliefs of its members, its assessment of the current state of assistance to adolescents who are pregnant or mothers, and the degree to which schools and community agencies are receptive to change. However, certain issues should be tackled at an early stage, either because they are basic to the effort to assist this population, or because they can be addressed without much difficulty, or both. At a minimum the group's recommendations should cover the following:

- developing equitable leave and absence policies for pregnant students and student who are mothers;

- organizing options for flexible scheduling;

- ensuring that the academic and support services at special programs for pregnant or parenting students are appropriate;

- designing sensible transfer policies for students attending special programs for a semester or two;

- developing staff in every school who can assist pregnant and parenting students and monitoring these students' school enrollment;

- allocating a proportion of dropout prevention or at-risk youth funding to identifying and counseling out-of-school young mothers;

- ensuring confidential advising for all pregnant and parenting students;

- developing mechanisms that facilitate the re-enrollment of teen mothers who are required to attend school under the new welfare legislation;

- providing some transportation help to young mothers who would otherwise find it very difficult to attend school and get their children to and from child care providers;

- establishing more child care facilities at school sites and improving assistance for students who want to use family day care providers in their own neighborhoods; and

- strengthening family planning education, counseling, and services.

Services that will probably have to be developed over a longer term because they require more ambitious planning and coalition building include a full-scale case-management system; alternative school programs for students with significant home responsibilities; guaranteed child care for mothers who want to earn their high school diplomas; employment-preparation programs especially geared to young mothers; school-based health clinics; and enriched programs for the children of teen mothers.

The next task is to recommend actions that address the problems the group has given highest priority. One way to organize the work is to draw up a work sheet for each priority area (see Figure 3).

Tackling a work sheet like this may help the group to organize its efforts, but being organized is, of course, only the beginning. The biggest challenge will be to fill in the category called Recommendations. Recognize, however, that the group need not develop recommendations in a vacuum. While efforts to strengthen attention to the educational needs of adolescent mothers and their children are at a rudimentary stage, a number of organizations have information on "best practices" and offer technical assistance to other groups (see the Appendix).

You can also order copies of the reports other communities have produced offering recommendations for how to improve educational opportunities for pregnant and parenting students.[97] In its report, the New York City Working Group calls upon the schools chancellor to "undertake an initiative to enable adolescent parents to meet their educational and parental responsibilities successfully" and urges the school system to make

---

97. Charles Cote, *Reading, Writing, and Raising Kids: A Study of Education and Services for Teen Parents in Rochester Schools* (Rochester, NY: Statewide Youth Advocacy, 1989).

FIGURE 3

MODEL WORK SHEET

Priority #1: Ensuring Confidential and Ongoing Guidance for Pregnant and Parenting Students

Question:

What sort of advising and ongoing guidance does the district provide for pregnant and parenting teens?

Answer:

Each teen is seen by a guidance counselor (caseload: one counselor for 210 students) or school social worker (caseload: one worker for 300 students), unless she transfers to the school for pregnant girls. For the two semesters the student typically spends there, she is followed by a social worker (caseload: 30). The social worker will help her return to her home school, but can provide no more assistance once the transfer is completed.

Goal:

To ensure that each mother-to-be and mother has access to a staff member who functions as a counselor, whose caseload is small, and who is specially trained to work with this population. This staff member should talk to each pregnant or parenting student in her caseload at least once a week to discuss the student's school progress and plans.

Short-term objective:

To develop a counselor/advocate service for pregnant and parenting students in two high schools that have been targeted for dropout prevention services.

Long-term objective:

To develop such a service in all middle and high schools, and to use the counselors as the first point of contact for staff in community agencies that are trying to re-enroll dropout mothers.

Agencies and district departments involved:

To plan and then implement a better guidance system, the school system, welfare department, health department, YWCA, and local settlement house should be involved.

Possible funding sources:

General school system funds, state at-risk youth funds, Carl Perkins Vocational Education funds, funds available to the welfare department through the Family Support Act, health department funds, Job Training Partnership Act funds.

Recommendations:

a five-year commitment to pursuing improvements at four institutional levels:

> *At the individual school level.* Unless the way individual schools respond to adolescent pregnancy and parenting can be changed, our efforts to help these students complete their education will remain peripheral to the system. All high school principals, and middle school principals where the need is concentrated, should plan and execute their school's approach to meeting the needs of pregnant and parenting students. This approach must include a written school plan, a broadly based advisory group, a meaningful and attractive educational program, flexible educational options, necessary support services, a designated school-based program coordinator, and a program of staff development.

> *At the regional or borough level.* A working infrastructure for stimulating and supporting building-level changes and the development of alternative ways to address the needs of pregnant and parenting students must be built at the field supervisory level. This infrastructure should consist of comprehensive regional Family Centers that provide a full-time program for pregnant and parenting students who wish to continue their education out of their "home" school and a variety of part-time programs for pregnant and parenting students in other school settings; these family centers should also serve as a resource to other schools and school districts throughout the system.

> *At the central Board of Education.* Clear and effective leadership from the top is critical. It should begin with the issuing of a Chancellor's policy statement and a statement of goals. In addition, the Chancellor should designate central staff to administer and oversee the initiative; to provide incentives, technical assistance and support; to continue planning based on an evaluation of the progress of this initiative; to secure necessary funding; and to integrate this policy into relevant new initiatives.

> *At the citywide interagency level.* Many citywide agencies and organizations, both public and private, need to develop working agreements about how best to jointly meet the educational needs of pregnant and parenting adolescents. These agreements should facilitate educational outreach to pregnant and parenting students using health facilities; collection of accurate data concerning the educational status of pregnant and parenting adolescents; better coordination of services and resources; and effective delivery of services to enable pregnant and parenting students to complete high school.[98]

---

98. Working Group on Educational Opportunities for Pregnant and Parenting Adolescents, *Helping Pregnant and Parenting Students Complete High School in New York City: Recommendations of the Chancellor's Working Group on Educational*

These recommendations are accompanied by an outline of implementation activities for the first year.

As the group begins to formulate its recommendations, the cochairs or their delegates should meet regularly with school district staff — from the superintendent's office, other departments, and individual schools. Such collaboration is essential. Staff members who will be needed to support proposals for change and cooperate with implementation should help the group develop sound plans for improvements in present policies and programs. In asking staff to join the group in formulating the recommendations, the group is, in effect, asking them to begin working on reforms. One of the cochairs of the Working Group in New York City summarizes the advantages of this approach: "Negotiating the final document was the way we negotiated the implementation."[99]

In developing recommendations, the group should make certain that it complements any other efforts already taking place in the community to develop interagency programs for pregnant and parenting teenagers. Also, the group will want to be certain that it has identified all possible sources of private or public funding. To offer teen mothers the array of services and opportunities they need, the school district will probably have to draw upon many funding streams.[100]

When the group has a list of specific recommendations, it will be ready to develop a report presenting them to the community. The report should take care to spell out the context in which the recommendations were developed: it should describe why and how the planning group was convened, the information the group gathered by assessing the needs of teenage mothers, and the process pursued in developing the recommendations.

The group should expect the entire process of writing a report to take at least six months. The work involved in revising drafts will probably extend over 2-4 months, as changes may take weeks to work out. The group will need to circulate at least three drafts of the report to group members.

Opportunities for Pregnant and Parenting Adolescents (New York: Center for Public Advocacy Research, 1989).

99. Warren, op. cit. (see note 93).

100. Denise Polit, *Building Self-Sufficiency: A Guide to Vocational and Employment Services for Teen Parents* (Saratoga, NY: Humanalysis, 1986).

Develop a preliminary draft for comment and a second draft incorporating these comments. Then ask the group to review a final draft for tone.

When the report is released, the next step is to distribute it to the superintendent, school board members, administrators in relevant public agencies, and other school and community leaders. Then arrange for meetings with appropriate administrators and staff members in both public and private agencies to discuss how to proceed with getting the recommendations put into practice.

The group might suggest to these administrators that members of the group work with the school district to establish an *implementation committee*, which would help the school district and community agencies pursue the recommendations. The committee should be composed of staff members from the school district and other relevant agencies and institutions, including top-level administrators, front-line staff members with first-hand knowledge of schools and programs most likely to be affected, and respected community activists and leaders. While some committee members should be drawn from the collaborative advisory group, others should be people who have not been involved to date but are critical to the success of the group's efforts. The first task of this committee would be to draw up *an implementation plan* including tasks, time lines, and lines of responsibility for pursuing changes. The committee should provide ongoing technical assistance to those involved with the implementation activities.

Another step toward establishing a climate conducive to reform efforts is to encourage the school district to articulate a clear policy statement on the education of pregnant and parenting teenagers. One city that has issued such a statement is Boston. In 1983 the Alliance for Young Families, a Boston teenage pregnancy coalition, organized a hearing for school board candidates on the educational needs of school-age parents. Staff of schools and community-based service agencies, as well as teenage parents, presented testimony. Shortly thereafter, a board member introduced a resolution to have a policy statement drafted by a group of experts from inside and outside the system. The superintendent appointed a working group to develop the statement, which was subsequently adopted. The full statement is presented in the Appendix as one illustration of how a school district might set a course for developing a system of support for school-age parents. Note that the statement covers considerably more ground than formal memoranda on districts' legal obligations to pregnant and parenting teens, which tend to concentrate on the most narrow interpretations of Title IX.

Monitoring Change

Even when the group's recommendations — or a modification of them — have been accepted by the school board or the superintendent, the group's work is not over: it should be prepared to monitor how the recommendations are being pursued by the implementation committee and later by school or agency departments and staff. Also, the group may want to ask a standing committee in your school district or community to take on responsibility for determining what kinds of recommendations for longer-term objectives are useful.

However the group organizes a plan to ensure ongoing attention to its recommendations, a few key educators and activists will need to meet periodically, take stock of what is happening, and identify unmet needs. An updated list of problems facing young mothers without high school diplomas or equivalency certificates should help define the agenda for teenage mothers in the community. When this group meets, undoubtedly it will also discover that certain aspects of the implementation plan are moving too slowly or are being altogether ignored. It may be necessary to reignite interest in the issues that originally moved officials to support the goals of the original advisory group. In other words, over time, the challenge may be to find new ways to highlight old problems.

Working in One School

If you are an individual educator interested in the problems of pregnant and parenting teens, you may be unable to persuade your entire school district to undertake reform. In the absence of support at the district level, try to initiate change in one school. Furthermore, even if districtwide changes are being planned, there is good reason to proceed with local school action, because early experiments with change at this level should shed light on how district reforms ought to be pursued.

Experience shows that building staff — principals, teachers, counselors, social workers, nurses, support staff — can all have a profound effect on the educational experiences of pregnant and parenting teenagers.[101] However, if your school has not yet begun to assist pregnant and parenting teens systematically, the degree to which staff members pay attention to the needs of this group may vary greatly. Your first task is to help the staff become more aware of the problems of teen mothers. Then you should work with staff who share your concern to develop and carry out plans for improving the treatment of these young women.

The elements of such plans and the steps you take to construct them are exactly the same as those described in the discussion on districtwide reform. Remember that in the school building, as in the district, it is important to defuse controversy by giving all interested parties a chance to express their views. Just as the district should seek out promising interventions for this population, so school-level planners should examine successful programs and activities in their school, in other schools in the district, elsewhere in their state, and around the nation. Conversely, if an individual school does achieve a workable new approach to retaining and re-enrolling young mothers-to-be and mothers, its staff members should try to encourage other educators in the community to learn from its experience.

*　　*　　*

This report began with profiles of three teenagers who faced significant obstacles to completing their education. Given the complexity of their life circumstances, even the most carefully constructed and supportive plan at the community, district, or school level may fail to make the difference in ensuring that they graduate and become self-sufficient. Still, a well-designed school-based approach to helping pregnant and parenting teens might give Lilia and her boyfriend the counseling they need to understand that marriage need not preclude continuing in school. Collaborative service delivery might offer Lilia some on-site child care to encourage her to stay in school after her baby is born. District policy reform might permit Keesha to continue in regular school, but under a less-rigid schedule — or, at least, it would give her strong guidance as she searches for an appropriate GED program or alternative school. New policies might allow

---

101. Nancy Compton, Mara Duncan and Jack Hruska, *How Schools Can Help Combat Student Pregnancy* (Washington, DC: National Education Association, 1987).

Melanie to continue working at the bakery by attending school part-time and might help her make prudent decisions about family planning.

Such efforts require good planning, and they require resources — both additional funds and staff energy. But if these or similar interventions are not tried, if schools continue to assume that the teenage parent must manage as best she can to finish school, and if other public agencies do not forge service partnerships with educational institutions, then both teenage mothers and their children will continue to be susceptible to economic hardship and the problems caused by poverty.

APPENDIX

NEW YORK CITY WORKING GROUP ON EDUCATIONAL OPPORTUNITIES FOR PREGNANT AND PARENTING ADOLESCENTS

In order to obtain the following documents on the New York City Working Group, send $10 to the Support Center for Educational Equity for Young Mothers, Academy for Educational Development, 100 Fifth Avenue, New York, New York 10011, (212) 243-1110.

1. *A Call to Action: Meeting the Educational Needs of Pregnant and Parenting Students in the New York City Public Schools*

2. The New York City Board of Education Chancellor's letter on the formation of the Working Group on Educational Opportunities for Pregnant and Parenting Adolescents

3. *Helping Pregnant and Parenting Students Complete High School in New York City: Recommendations of the Chancellor's Working Group on Educational Opportunities for Pregnant and Parenting Adolescents*

RESOURCE ORGANIZATIONS

The following organizations offer publications, information, or technical assistance on policies and programs for improving educational opportunities for pregnant and parenting teenagers.

Academy for Educational Development: Support Center for Educational Equity for Young Mothers
100 Fifth Avenue
New York, New York 10011
212-243-1110
Contact: Michele Cahill or Constancia Warren

Alliance for Young Families
8 Kingston Street
Boston, Massachusetts 02111
617-482-9122
Contact: Joan Tigue

Children's Defense Fund: Adolescent Pregnancy Prevention Clearinghouse
122 C Street N.W.
Washington, DC 20001
202-628-8787
Contact: Ray O'Brien or Sharon Adams Taylor

Council of Chief State School Officers: Joining Forces
400 N. Capital Street, Suite 379
Washington, DC 20001
202-393-8159
Contact: Janet Levy

Family Service Agency of San Francisco:
Teenage Pregnancy and Parenting Project
1325 Florida Street
San Francisco, California
415-648-8810
Contact: Amy Loomis

Morning Glory Press
6595 San Haroldo Way
Buena Park, California 90620
714-828-1998
Contact: Jeanne Lindsay

National Association of State Boards of Education:
Counselor/Advocate Project
1012 Cameron Street
Alexandria, Virginia 22314
703-684-4000
Contact: Janice Earle

National Organization on Adolescent
Pregnancy and Parenting
P.O. Box 2365
Reston, Virginia 22090
703-435-3948
Contact: Kathleen Sheeran

New Futures School
5400 Cutler Street, N.E.
Albuquerque, New Mexico 87110
505-883-5680
Contact: Caroline Gaston

New York City Board of Education Dropout Prevention Program Services Linkage Project for Parenting Adolescents
122 Amsterdam Avenue, Room 387-9
New York, New York 10023
212-874-4990
Contact: Juliet Ucelli

**Wellesley College Center for Research on Women:
Increasing Educational Opportunities for Young Parents
 and Their Children Project**
Wellesley, Massachusetts 02181
617-235-0320, ext. 2558
Contact: Fern Marx

STUDENT REVIEW

These are guidelines for answering the four questions listed in Figure 1.

1. *How many pregnant teenagers (who are going to term) and teenage mothers live in the community?*

It is unlikely that anyone in the community will have the answer to this question. The group will have to calculate an answer by adding together an estimate of the *total number of teenage mothers living in your community* as of the latest year for which birth data are available and an estimate of the *number of teenagers who were pregnant with their first baby in that same year, but who delivered the following year.* Here are two steps to take for developing these estimates.

> *Step 1: Calculate the total number of teenage mothers living in the community.*

Focusing on the latest year in which the group can obtain birth data for the community — for example, 1987 — the group must determine:

- *The number of teenagers who became mothers for the first time in 1987.* Obtain data on the number of births to teenagers in the community in 1987. The local health department should have annual data on the number of babies born to mothers aged 19 and younger. However, the number of births to teenagers in any given year is greater than the number of teenagers who became first-time mothers that year. Nationally, about 25 percent of births to teenagers occur to women who already have one or more children. If the department cannot provide figures on births to first-time teenage mothers, reduce the total number of births to teen mothers in 1987 by 25 percent.

- *The number of young women who gave birth in earlier years and were still teenagers in 1987.* The group should be able to obtain teenage birth data broken down by age groups, so that it can review the age-specific birth figures for teenagers during the preceding five years in the community. If age-specific birth data is not available for any of the previous years, use the corresponding numbers for 1987, since they are likely to be reasonably similar (unless the community has been unusually successful with pregnancy prevention or the teenage abortion rate has risen sharply). Also, if the group cannot obtain data on first-time mothers, use the age-specific birth data and reduce the number of mothers who were 18 in 1987 by 25 percent, because some of these mothers were having their second child. Then add together the data collected for these five categories:

1. The first-time mothers who were 18 or younger in 1986
2. The first-time mothers who were 17 or younger in 1985
3. The first-time mothers who were 16 or younger in 1984
4. The first-time mothers who were 15 or younger in 1983
5. The first-time mothers who were 14 or younger in 1982

Now add the sum of these numbers to the number of first-time mothers in 1987 that you calculated earlier. This should yield a reasonable estimate of how many adolescent mothers lived in the community in 1987.

Step 2: Calculate the number of teenagers who were pregnant with their first baby in 1987, but who delivered the following year. Assume that the number of pregnant teens in this category is about the same as the number of teenagers who gave birth to their first child in 1987.

Now add the total of all teenage mothers in 1987 (from Step 1) to the number of teenagers who were pregnant with their first baby in that year, but who delivered the following year (from Step 2). This yields a rough estimate of the number of pregnant and parenting teenagers in the community in 1987.

2. *What proportion of these pregnant girls and young mothers have not completed high school?*

As discussed earlier, over half of all teenage mothers have not completed high school. Therefore, the group can probably assume that this is the situation in its community. Furthermore, the group can assume that the proportion of pregnant teens who are going to term and have not graduated yet is similar to the proportion of teenage mothers who have not finished school.

However, the group can try to acquire local data. Ask if the local or state

Department of Vital Statistics collects information on teenage mothers' educational attainment in the course of aggregating data from birth certificates. If this information is not collected, find out if it is recorded on teenage mothers' charts when they give birth at local hospitals. (A large proportion of teenage mothers will deliver at public hospitals or at other hospitals that accept Medicaid patients.) Ask staff at a local hospital to review a representative sample of charts and estimate the rate of high school completion among teenage mothers who gave birth there.

3. *Among pregnant teens and teen mothers who do not have a high school diploma, what proportion are pursuing their education either through the school system or through a GED program?*

To answer this question, poll the school district and local service providers for information on how many pregnant and parenting teens they are assisting with educational services. Then compare this figure with your estimate of the number of pregnant and parenting teens who need to complete high school. The group should recognize, however, that relying solely on statistics on teens currently receiving services may leave it with an overly positive picture of the educational prospects for teen parents in its community. This is because not all of the young women now enrolled in an educational program will graduate. Some will drop out and are likely to need special encouragement to return and graduate.

4. *What proportion of pregnant students and young mothers without a high school diploma need academic course work that is not at the high school level (middle-school-level course work or other specialized educational services)?*

No single data source will be available to supply this information. The group will need to interview service providers and educators who work with pregnant and parenting teens to arrive at estimates of how many of these teens have educational needs that make course work at the high school level inappropriate for them.

SERVICE REVIEW

You will find here a more complete set of questions to help you gather as much information as you can to answer the five questions listed in Figure 2.

1. *What are the school district policies, programs, and practices that are explicitly directed to pregnant and parenting students?*

   - How does the district *identify pregnant or parenting students and track their educational progress*? Who is responsible for providing advice about educational options? How is confidentiality maintained? How is ongoing counseling provided? Is case-management care offered? Does each school have a staff advocate/counselor designated to help pregnant and parenting students? What are the caseloads of these staff members?

   - How does the district ensure *academic continuity* among pregnant students or young mothers? Can teenagers elect develop an individual education plan for a shortened day at school? Does the district offer home tutoring for pregnant students or new mothers?

   - Does the district operate *special programs* for pregnant students or young mothers? If so, what is the quality of the academic components of these programs? Are pregnant or parenting students encouraged to attend these special programs? If so, are students also aware that they do not have to attend them, but can continue in their mainstream schools?

     If a student attends a special program does she take a leave of absence from her home school, or must she make a formal transfer? What kinds of procedures are involved for a student and her family if she must make a formal transfer? Who monitors whether teens who apply for transfers carry through on their intentions to attend a special school? Who monitors whether these same teenagers complete the transfer back from the special school? Does tracking or monitoring include reentry support — staff who welcome students back to school and help them stay in school?

     What is the maximum length of time a pregnant or parenting teen can remain in a special program? Is it sufficiently long to allow the staff to develop supportive, ongoing relationships with her?

   - How are *leave and absence policies* applied to pregnant and parenting students? What constitutes a valid medical excuse? How long is the maternity leave period granted to a new mother? Is the amount of time comparable to that offered mothers in other institutions — in the workplace, for instance? What is the school's response if a mother needs more time? What if a young mother must miss school for a child's illness or for other parenting responsibilities, including appointments with the welfare department?

- What *support services* does the district offer to pregnant and parenting teens in special schools? In mainstream schools? Specifically:

  What health services are available? Are there health education classes tailored to the needs of pregnant and parenting students? Are they credit-bearing classes? Are school-based health clinics available? At which schools? What help is offered to young mothers so they are able to secure health services for themselves or for their children? Since young mothers are at high risk for a second, often unplanned, pregnancy within two years of their first birth, what steps are being taken to assist them with family planning?

  What types of *child care services* or assistance in locating such services are available? At which schools?

  Are young mothers who wish to bring children to school provided assistance in locating good *transportation* to do so?

  Do young mothers have access to classes on and help with *parenting education*?

- Overall, *are the district's services and policies* for pregnant and parenting teens *more responsive to the needs of students who are pregnant* than to the needs of young mothers? Does assistance *focus more on medical and social needs* than on academic ones?

- Does the *school district work collaboratively with other public agencies and community institutions* to assist teenage mothers and mothers-to-be? What types of services are provided this way?

- *What information about pregnant and parenting teens and about services for this group is routinely collected* in your school district and in your community? What other information is needed? (The group should be able to answer this last question by reflecting on its own experience in trying to gather local data on pregnant and parenting teenagers and services for them.)

2. *What policies, programs, and practices of the school system that are not explicitly aimed at pregnant and parenting teenagers nevertheless have significant effects on their educational experiences?*

Are there a range of educational options that pregnant and parenting students can comfortably and successfully use, including the possibility of instruction in alternative schools, night schools, employment preparation programs, adult education and GED classes? Is flexible scheduling available? Are leave and absense policies too rigid?

Are dropout prevention or at-risk youth initiatives being used to support work with pregnant and parenting students? Have they been used to reach mothers who have not completed high school? Are these efforts informal, or are they organized and systematic?

3. *How do staff members treat pregnant and parenting students?*

If, as is likely, there is some controversy about how to handle education for this group, what is the district doing to strengthen staff development — to help school staff express their views on these issues, acquire more information about the problem of adolescent pregnancy, and improve their skills in working with student mothers and mothers-to-be?

4. *What efforts are being made in the district to ensure that the children of teenage mothers will be adequately prepared to enter school?*

Does the district target the children of teen mothers for any special services? Is there a possibility that any existing programs to increase school success among student mothers might have an adverse effect on their children? For instance, are young mothers being encouraged to continue their education, but not being given adequate assistance to secure good child care arrangements? Or does the district try to attract more young mothers into work preparation experiences without taking into account how these experiences should be structured so that student mothers are not away from their children for longer than they feel comfortable leaving them? Similarly, be sure to consider if any changes the group recommends take these children's needs into account.

5. *What are the strengths and shortcomings of the school district's policies, programs, and practices just reviewed?*

THE BOSTON SCHOOL COMMITTEE POLICY STATEMENT ON SCHOOL-AGE PARENTS

December 13, 1983

The Boston School Committee supports the development of a full range of academic and support services programs for school-age parents and parents-to-be in the Boston Public Schools. The School Committee believes that such programs are needed in order to assist and encourage all students to achieve the academic and vocational skills required to reach their maximum potential.

The School Committee encourages school-age parents and parents-to-be to continue their education in the least restrictive setting while receiving health, social service and day-care services. Efforts to maximize their educational participation shall be a cooperative undertaking between the School Department and community agencies providing services to this population. No Boston Public School student shall be systematically excluded from educational participation because of pregnancy. Efforts to serve pregnant teens and young school-age parents shall focus on both students who have dropped out of school and students who are enrolled in the Boston Public Schools. Community agencies shall be made aware of the School Committee policy in an effort to identify those students that have dropped out due to their parenting obligations.

Accordingly, the following guidelines are established:

1. Pregnant students and school-age parents are encouraged to remain in school as long as possible but may be permitted two options: (a) to apply for a leave of absence with the approval of the Headmaster/ Principal of the school in which the student is enrolled, or (b) to apply for a limited leave of absence. During the limited leave, parenting students who initiate and maintain contact with their assigned school and teachers and who meet course requirements for academic achievement shall be marked as "constructively present." It is the re-

69

sponsibility of the individual school to offer the opportunity to make up missed work. If a student is in need of home instruction for verifiable medical reasons, it shall be provided.

2. A school-age parent shall be deemed "constructively present" if she cannot attend school on a given day due to the verifiable illness of her child or as a result of pre/postnatal complications. Such verification shall require a doctor's certification.

3. The use of flexible scheduling, including options such as flexible campus and summer/evening school enrollment, shall be encouraged to accommodate the student's parenting responsibilities.

4. The School Department supports existing programs and the establishment of new programs for pregnant students and school-age parents such as competency- based diploma programs, Graduate Equivalency Diploma (GED), external diploma programs, and off-site educational programs such as community-based educational programs.

5. The School Department shall develop and implement a sex education curriculum for all grade levels in accordance with approved policy. The School Department shall institute a family life skills curriculum as part of the science and /or health curriculum. In conjunction with the family life skills curriculum, internship components at daycare centers will be explored.

For more information, contact the Alliance for Young Families, 8 Kingston Street, Boston, MA 02111, 617-482-9122.